The "Zero's Journey"

iContractor 2.0

The "Zero's Journey"

iContractor 2.0

A Modern-day Survival Guide to Weathering Accidental Enlightenment

jon

The "Zero's Journey" – iContractor 2.0 – A Modern-day Survival Guide to Weathering Accidental Enlightenment by jon

© 2013, 2014 by **Jon M. Ketcham**. All rights reserved.

No part of this publication may be reproduced or transmitted in any form or by any means, mechanical or electronic, including photocopying and recording, or by any information storage and retrieval system, without permission in writing from author or publisher. The exception would be in the case of brief quotations embodied in the critical articles or reviews and pages where permission is specifically granted by the publisher or author.

Disclaimer: The Publisher and the Author make no representations or warranties with respect to the accuracy or completeness of the contents of this work and specifically disclaim all warranties, including without limitation warranties of fitness for a particular purpose. The fact that an organization or website is referred to in this work as a citation and/or a potential source of further information does not mean that the Publisher or the Author endorses the information the organization or website may provide or recommendations it may make. Further, readers should be aware that internet websites listed in this work may have changed or disappeared between when this work was written and when it is read. Please see following page for additional disclaimer.

ABIYD Publishing Company
765 Park Ave
Meadville, PA 16335
www.ABIYD.com

Illustrations by: Jon D. Ketcham & Jon M. Ketcham

ISBN: 978-0-9905511-0-2 cloth
ISBN: 978-0-9905511-2-6 paperback
Library of Congress Control Number: 2014911800

10 9 8 7 6 5 4 3 2 1

Motivational & Inspirational / Metaphysics / Mysticism

First Edition Printed in the United States.

Additional Disclaimer

The information and strategies provided by **The "Zero's Journey"** are intended to educate, inform, empower, amuse and inspire you on your personal journey towards excellence: goal-setting/goal-achieving, growing your business/bank account, achieving optimal health/wellness, improving your relationships and maximizing your quality of life. It is clearly not intended to replace a one-on-one relationship with a licensed health care professional and it is definitely not offered up as a substitute for proper medical or chiropractic advice, diagnosis or treatment. Proper diagnosis and advice relative to treatment of any existing health conditions cannot be made through a book and is well beyond the scope of any information offered. The intent of the author is solely to offer information of a general nature to assist you on your quest for spiritual and emotional well-being. The author will not accept any liability, perceived or otherwise, for the improper application of any principles taught through this text. In the event you, the reader, choose to use or apply any of the strategies in this book for yourself, which is your constitutional right, the author and the publisher assume no responsibility for your actions.

Weathering Accidental Enlightenment

Dedication

To my Mom, deceased thirty-two years now, and my Dad, deceased nearly ten years; both of you gone from the physical plane yet ever near to my heart. You always loved and supported me in the pursuit of my afflatus. Writing <u>The "Zero's Journey"</u> led me to a much deeper understanding of your own battles with the Dark Nights. Mom, you used to refer to me as the "Bright Spot" in your day. Perhaps my current insights could have eased your painful journey. If my writing can help to ease the journey for even one fellow traveler, I will have succeeded in my goal for this work.

Weathering Accidental Enlightenment

Table of Contents

Disclaimers — *iv, v*

Dedication — *vii*

Table of Contents — *ix*

A Couple Quick Notes Pertaining To The Quotes — *xiii*

Preface — *xv*

Introduction – by Jacob Nordby — *xix*

Chapter 1   Reflector Vector –
Deconstructing the "Law of Attraction"   1

Chapter 2   StairWELL to Success…
Steps and More Steps   11

Chapter 3   Finding Your AFFLATUS…
Constructing Your Magnificent "Why"   25

Weathering Accidental Enlightenment

Chapters 4 – 11 **AFFLATUS:**

Chapter 4 **AFFLATUS** – Attitude	43
Chapter 5 **AFFLATUS** – Faith	51
Chapter 6 **AFFLATUS** – Financial Consciousness	61
Chapter 7 **AFFLATUS** – Laughter	71
Chapter 8 **AFFLATUS** – Allowing	75
Chapter 9 **AFFLATUS** -Thanksgiving	89
Chapter 10 **AFFLATUS** - U.S.P. "Unique Selling Proposition"	93
Chapter 11 **AFFLATUS** – Service	101
Chapter 12 Walking in Silence — Solitary Refinement	105
Chapter 13 Weathering the "Dark Nights" — A Tale of Two Survivors	113
Chapter 14 The Coming of the Dawn	129
Chapter 15 The "Zero's Journey"	135

Afterward: Crossing the "Fault Line"   *147*

Epilogue: 20¢ worth of Philosophy
1 Year Later   *149*

About the Author   *157*

Connecting to Dr. Ketcham   *161*

Appendix A: Constructive Concepts: Words
to live by from The "Zero's Journey"   *163*

Appendix B: The "Safety Pin Cycle"
– re-visited   *187*

Appendix C: Being About One's
Purpose For Being   *199*

Appendix D: Pre-History
Thoughts & Musings   *209*

Appendix E: Required Reading List
— 3 Plus One   *213*

Permissions   *217*

Sources   *221*

Bibliography   *243*

Weathering Accidental Enlightenment

Notes   *255*

A Couple Quick Notes Pertaining To The Quotes

The man who never reads will never be read; he who never quotes will never be quoted. He who will not use the thoughts of other men's brains, proves that he has no brains of his own.
Charles Spurgeon (1)

Anyone familiar with my writing style knows that I LOVE quotes!!! I have tried my utmost to give credit where credit is due. If I have inadvertently indicated an erroneous source or failed to indicate a source where I should have, I apologize ahead of time for my oversight. However, **none** of the quotes I have chosen for this volume were picked based upon *who said what*. Rather, they were each carefully selected based solely upon *what was actually said*. Furthermore, my inclusion of any given author's quote does not in any way suggest that they in any way support my message or manner of use. In your reading of this tome, try to focus primarily on the message contained in each poetic contribution more so than on each specific poet.

  Among the sources that I have quoted, the Bible has probably been cited the most often. Many revere the Bible as the "inspired word of God" and I most certainly concur with that sentiment. However, I do not believe that the Bible is the only work containing the inspired word of God. In fact, in my humble opinion, anytime someone is in tune with their own Divinity and following their own afflatus, their work is going to be "inspired." That is not to say that any of the inspired works of mankind are without flaw. Even when driven from the depths of our own afflatus, we still filter everything we create, the Bible included, through the windows of bias that are our attitudes, perceptions and worldview.

Additionally, authors throughout the centuries have used a variety of different titles and analogies to all refer to the same solitary, supreme force from which everyone and everything emanates. These titles have included (in alphabetical order): the Creator, the desert, Divinity, God, Heaven, Life, Lord Krishna, Love, Source and the Universe. All of the aforementioned titles appear in this text at one point or another and can be used interchangeably.

Preface

Each man (is) the architect of his own fortune.
Appius Claudius Caecus (1)

Some write and speak because they like to see their name in print and hear themselves talk. That is not the case for me. In fact, by nature, I am quite introverted and shy away from any type of public interactions. I write and speak, however, because I have been fortunate enough to find and follow my own afflatus. I write and speak because I have a message burning inside of me, a message so powerful that it will consume me from within if I don't acquiesce and let it out to be shared with others, others just like you!

I won't pretend to have all, or even any, of the answers. I don't! I just write about life, as seen through the filter of my own experiences, as I have come to understand it. And, that understanding is subject to change.

When I wrote iContractor 1, I said all that I had to say at that time. And, while iContractor 1 was not a particularly long book, I think it met the standard set by Nietzsche who said, "It is my ambition to say in ten sentences what everyone else says in a whole book — what everyone else does not say in a whole book." (2) Since that time,

Weathering Accidental Enlightenment

my understanding has grown and deepened exponentially. I found that I have more to say after all.

Most people have not found their afflatus; most people do not believe in their dreams. In fact, most people are at a complete loss for direction, they don't know themselves; they are sorely lacking confidence, they don't love themselves and they are lacking capabilities, struggling to improve themselves but not making any headway. And, for those who have found their afflatus, many succumb to the "night terrors" of the Dark Night of the Soul.

Reading The "Zero's Journey" will **not** teach you how to become a millionaire in six weeks, how to find true love without any effort or how to accomplish all of your dreams by just wishing. What it will do is help you to find your direction, assist you in developing your self-confidence and guide you to productively improving your capabilities. If you find yourself lost, wandering blindly through the Dark Night, The "Zero's Journey" will help to illuminate a path for your dream fulfillment.

You are held back, like a prisoner in shackles, by anything you do not understand. Hopefully, after reading The "Zero's Journey",

The Zero's Journey

you will come to a full understanding and appreciation of the fact that you already possess everything you are currently in search of, everything you think you need to live the life of your dreams. All of the power and magic that exist in the Universe are already perfectly reflected in your very being at this very moment. Once you get your inner house in order, constructing your dream life will take care of itself.

Weathering Accidental Enlightenment

Introduction

There is a Shadow Wolf which pursues us all our lives. We run from it and use every possible shield to defend ourselves against it— careers, money, relationships, position, possessions. As long as we can fend it off, we pretend to not be afraid of this pursuer.

For some, the day comes when we can no longer run. We must turn and face our nemesis. The Shadow Wolf overtakes us at last and we are swallowed by what we feared the most. We discover that the only thing this terrifying creature wanted was to require that we ask the question: "Who really am I?". Those of us fortunate enough to be forced by life into a box canyon from which we cannot run are given a great gift. We are shown that nothing external can define or devour us. Who We Really Are cannot be dented, scratched or diminished in any way.

From this dark night of the soul, we can emerge as beings aware of our wholeness and power in a new way. We can go forth in the world with a profound sense of purpose, joy and playfulness. We are free to experiment, experience and fail. We are free to embrace and accept success on every level.

Weathering Accidental Enlightenment

Dr. Jon Ketcham reveals this path in this book. Unlike so many popular teachers of modern psycho-spirituality, he begins at the core with an understanding that we must first know ourselves and be in touch with our own deepest desires rather than seek to fill the void with all the external markers of success.

As you read this book and use the tools it offers, know that you are experiencing the work of a man who has first walked through hell and now comes back to share how he learned to create a beautiful new reality. This is first-hand, priceless information offered by a fellow traveler who will only share what he has embodied.

If you are walking through your own dark night of the soul and wondering whether or not the light will ever shine again, take courage! The wisdom in these pages is forged in the author's own fire of fear, desperation and transformation.

Jacob Nordby
Author
"The Divine Arsonist: a tale of awakening"

Chapter 1

Reflector Vector – Deconstructing the "Law of Attraction"

par ♦ a ♦ digm - noun

a philosophical and theoretical framework of a scientific school or discipline within which theories, laws and generalizations and the experiments performed in support of them are formulated (1)

Paradigms are used to provide a reference framework from which to understand our Universe and then, hopefully, to successfully predict which outcomes will follow any given course of action or circumstance. Thomas Kuhn, author of <u>The Structure of Scientific Revolutions</u> states, "Paradigms gain their status because they are more successful than their competitors in solving a few problems that the group of practitioners has come to recognize as acute." (2) He continues, "Because it demands large-scale paradigm destruction and major shifts in the problems and techniques of normal science, the emergence of new theories is generally preceded by a period of pronounced professional insecurity." (3) "During the transition

Weathering Accidental Enlightenment

period there will be a large but never complete overlap between the problems that can be solved by the old and by the new paradigm. But, there will also be a decisive difference in the modes of solution." (4)

For illustrative purposes, let's consider the field of astronomy. The Ptolemaic system was considered the law of the land for nearly seventeen centuries; from two centuries before Christ until the early 1600s. Many civilizations, including ancient Greece, relied on this geocentric model which had at its core a belief that the earth was the stationary center of our solar system and all of the other celestial bodies, including the sun, revolved around it. Critical to its long duration was its considerable success in predicting the changing positions of both the planets and the stars.

During the late 1500s and early 1600s, the Copernican system came to light. Copernicus felt that the sun was the center of the solar system and the earth, along with the rest of the planets, revolved around it. And while, thanks to the efforts of Galileo, the Copernican system eventually replaced the Ptolemaic system, "for the stars, Ptolemaic astronomy is still widely used today as an engineering approximation; for the planets, Ptolemy's predictions were as good as Copernicus'." (5) For his efforts, Copernicus' book was initially ignored and later banned. Galileo, for his part in bringing the work of Copernicus to the masses, was condemned to hell.

First they ignore you. Then they ridicule you.
And then they attack you and want to burn you.
And then they build monuments to you.
Nicholas Klein (6)

This brings us to our discussion today concerning the Law of Attraction. In my humble opinion, the classic works of Ralph Waldo Trine [In Tune With The Infinite] (7), Wallace Wattles [The Science of Getting Rich] (8), Charles Haanel [The Master Key System] (9), Napoleon Hill [Think And Grow Rich] (10), Rhonda Byrne [The Secret] (11) and even myself [iContractor 1] (12) are **all** slightly off-base, missing the final obvious, yet subtle, conclusion that there is no such thing as the Law of Attraction! None whatsoever!

Nowhere in the natural world does "like attract like." Even a cursory review of any college-level physics textbook will reveal this. The forces that magnets exert upon one another are such that **like poles repel** one another and opposite poles attract one another. Like and opposite electric charges can be seen to behave similarly. Even in chemistry and physiology, solutes in solution diffuse from high concentrations to low concentrations (opposites moving toward each other) until equilibrium is reached (likes, side by side) at which point **nothing** further occurs. As such, the Law of "Attraction" is really a misnomer since like does not attract like.

Another point of conflict contained within the Law of Attraction comes from its underlying implication that anyone is lacking in any way, thus necessitating the power to "attract" anything in the first place. In the Bible, Luke 17:21 states, "the kingdom of God is within you." (13) Psalm 23 states, "I shalt not want... my cup runneth over." (14) Clearly, if "the kingdom of God is within you" AND you "shalt not want" because your "cup runneth over" then there is incongruency here because you cannot be lacking in any way. Similarly, in the sacred Hindu text, The Bhagavad-Gita, Lord Krishna states, "the lord resides in the heart of all creatures." (15) Sanjaya then summarizes, also in The Bhagavad-Gita, "Where Krishna is... there do fortune, victory, abundance ... exist." (16) And, according to Tibetan Buddhist precepts, "The secret wisdom of the Dzogchen teaches us that whatever we are looking for, it is always right here... what we seek, we already are." (17)

In spite of its seemingly miraculous ability to help some people to improve their station in life, the Law of Attraction is based upon principles that defy the known laws of physics, chemistry and physiology AND that deny the word of God (and numerous other spiritual teachers and teachings, including sacred Hindu texts and Tibetan Buddhist precepts); based on these two flawed assumptions: like attracts like and you are lacking in some way. And, for all the success stories, there are millions more who *believe* in the Law of Attraction, struggle to attract their desires and still come up empty-handed. Why? The Law of Attraction cannot possibly be an accurate depiction of reality!

> *That which has always been accepted by everyone, everywhere, is almost certain to be false.*
> Paul Valéry (18)

There may be no such thing as the Law of Attraction BUT perhaps there is a Law of *Reflection*. Maybe it is not about what you are "attracting" to you. Instead, what if it is all about what you are putting out there that ultimately gets "reflected" back to you? Like may not attract like but like DOES reflect like! Imagine shining a flashlight at a mirror in a darkened room. The light you shine gets reflected back to you. Think of a smile. If you go out into the world trying to "attract" a smile, all the while frowning, you won't likely attract another smile. In fact, you will probably frighten people. However, if you go out in public and just smile, genuinely, at others, many

Weathering Accidental Enlightenment

will smile back at you, reflecting your smile back to you from multiple directions; the Law of Reflection!

Borrowing from <u>iContractor 1</u>, Genesis 1:27 states, "God created man in His own image." (19) John 8:12 states, "I am the light of the world. He who follows Me shall not walk in darkness, but have the light of life." (20) John 10:30 continues, "I and My Father are one." (21) Separation from God is often described as "being in the dark." Survivors of near-death experiences all talk about going towards or returning to the light. When people figure out the solution to a long perplexing problem, they often say they have "seen the light." The truth is, we are all beings of light; light resonating with a dense vibrational form. (22) The problem, however, is that most of us have forgotten who we really are! Lama Surya Das, the most highly trained American lama in the Tibetan tradition, tells us that, "A beautiful Tibetan prayer wishes that we may all together reach enlightenment that we may all find the Buddha within and awaken to who and what we really are... We are all lit up from within as if from a sacred source." (23)

There is an old Hawaiian Molokai parable that says we come into this world as bowls of radiant light. As we express negative emotions like anger, fear, jealousy and resentment, we gradually fill our bowls full of rocks until our light is barely visible. Only by carefully choosing your responses to any and every given set of circumstances can you release your negative emotions, dump your rocks and re-experience your light.

Consider this, if we are all spiritual beings of light and whatever we emit is what gets reflected back to us via the Law of Reflection, doesn't it make sense to focus more on who you are being on the inside, what you are emitting, than what you think is missing on the outside that you think you must attract? Contrary to what the Law of Attraction suggests, perhaps we do not send out our thoughts, feeling/emotions and actions as vibrations that go out and *find* "like" things and bring them back to us. Rather, maybe who you are being on the inside shines outward and gets reflected back to you from the mirror of God, on a massive, magnified scale, as the people, events and circumstances of your life through the Law of Reflection.

The Game of Life is a game of boomerangs.
Man's thoughts, deeds and words return to him,
sooner or later, with astounding accuracy.
Florence Scovel Shinn (24)

Weathering Accidental Enlightenment

If you find yourself in want it is likely because you have forgotten who you are. I keep coming back to this point because it is imperative that you grasp its significance. We all come from the light. "God created man in His own image." (25) We are reflections of God. Thus, we too are the light. Sometimes, we surround ourselves with darkness so we can get to know who we really are. After all, a candle in the sunshine is sometimes difficult to perceive. This is how serious illness, calamity and orientation issues can serve to put us in touch with our own true nature: by "forcing" us to grapple with the big questions of life. But, know this too. We all come from abundance. It is who we are. It too is our nature. Again, Psalm 23 says, "I shalt not want... my cup runneth over." (26) It is impossible to be lacking in any way unless we ourselves make it so. We have enough already. We are enough already!

You can never out-dark the light. Even the smallest candle is more powerful than the deepest night.
Jacob Nordby (27)

This is why practicing "gratitude in advance" is so powerful. It enables us to embrace the fact that, whatever it is that we want, we **already** have it. And THAT is what gets reflected back to us!

The Zero's Journey

Jim Rohn, "America's Foremost Business Philosopher" used to say that you become like the five people you spend the most time around. The Law of Reflection brings instant clarity to this. Who we surround ourselves with affects who we reflect and who reflects us. The more negative influences we are reflecting back to others, the less our own light can shine through.

The simple 3-step process, as outlined in iContractor 1 and the following chapter, is still a great way to get clear on who you are and create the life of your dreams. But don't get too hung up on what specific ways your dream will manifest. You cannot control where your "reflections" will be shown to you from, nor when. Focus on "WHAT" you want, see it as already accomplished. Feel it! Be it! Emanate it! Give thanks for it! Then let God decide where and when and how it gets reflected back to you. Your attitudes and emotions color and can block your light. You maximize your light by being true to you.

Whatever you ask for in prayer, believe that you have received it, and it will be yours.
Bible (28)

Light travels at a fixed speed, the speed of light. Some of the stars you see in the night sky are no longer in existence, but their light is just

Weathering Accidental Enlightenment

now reaching us. Likewise, there are stars whose light has yet to reach us. Don't get caught up on the speed of light or the speed and direction of its reflection. Know this, you already have everything you need inside of you. The sooner you recognize this, the sooner you will emit it via your thoughts, feelings/emotions and actions. And then, that is what will get reflected back to you as the people, events and circumstances of your life through the Law of Reflection.

Chapter 2

StairWELL to Success...
Steps and More Steps

Not to know the things you ought to know is illness.
Lao Tzu (1)

According to recent reports, the self-help/self-improvement industry is a $10 billion per year business. More people than ever are on a seemingly desperate mission to change their lives for the better. Yet, I would posit that 98% of them are doomed to fail for lack of an understanding that lasting, positive change and growth requires an essential, sequential, 3-step process. Missing one or two of the essential, sequential steps, much like missing one or two pieces of a 3-piece puzzle, prevents its successful completion. That helps explain why, with more money than ever being spent on self-improvement, unemployment rates, divorce rates and suicide rates, rather than declining, are at all-time record high levels.

This essential, sequential, 3-step process is as follows:

- **Step one:** Know Yourself

Weathering Accidental Enlightenment

- **Step two:** Love Yourself

- **Step three:** Improve Yourself

Know Yourself

There are three things extremely hard: steel, a diamond and to know one's self.
Benjamin Franklin (2)

In ancient Greece, the temple was set up such that there were two parts: an outer part that was open to the beginning initiates and an inner part that was reserved solely for those who proved to be worthy of acquiring higher knowledge and insight. In the inner temple, there were written many proverbs, one of which stated, "Man know thyself... and thou shalt know the gods." (3) Some in Greece believed Apollo himself had delivered this advice. Plato gave rightful import to the phrase when he stated, "People make themselves appear ridiculous when they are trying to know obscure things before they know themselves;" wise advice indeed. (4)

How many people actually take the time to ponder the big questions: "Who am I? Why am I here? What do I stand for?" Unless forced by circumstance to delve into such matters, most are content to evade the magnitude of such weighty ponderings. Fortunate indeed are those individuals who, whether due to serious illness, calamity or orientation, are pushed early on in life to consider such magnificent questions.

Knowing yourself is the beginning of all wisdom.
Aristotle (5)

If you asked someone to define themselves by asking, "Who are you?" you would likely get a series of answers that could easily be fit into one of five categories: what they *do* (activity roles: husband/wife, boyfriend/girlfriend, father/mother, occupation, hobbies), what they *did* ("trophy" roles: degrees, awards, accolades, prior accomplishments), how they *look* (physical attributes: based on height, weight, body-type, nationality, gender, race), what they *believe* (ideologies: religious, philosophical, political) or what they *have* (physical possessions: homeowner/renter, business owner, fancy car/boat/etc.). Most people develop very constipated, restrictive views of themselves based upon these labels that they then use to define and confine their capabilities. But, according to the Bible, Genesis 1:27 clearly states, "God created man in His own image." (6) As such, we are all "reflections" of God! Pierre Teilhard de Chardin, French philosopher and Jesuit priest states, "We are not human beings having a spiritual experience. We are spiritual beings having a human experience." (7)

In light of this, two things should become readily apparent: first, we are not limited in our capabilities in any way other than those limits we create for ourselves and second, any longings, desires, passions, interests and talents we have are, as reflections of God, meant to be celebrated and utilized, not stifled and constricted. In fact, denying our innermost longings is denying God Himself! So, this begs the question anew. Who are you? Maybe it's time you made the time to really find out! What are your interests? Talents? Strengths? Weaknesses? Flaws? Start by making a list. Make several lists, "My top 100 strengths are...," "My top 100 weaknesses are...."

Understand this, trying to improve yourself without first knowing yourself is like wanting to plan a trip to a foreign country but without regard for where you will be starting from. Where do you start? What modes of travel will be necessary? How do you assess your progress? Only by first knowing where you are at can you then create a workable strategy to get to where you want to go.

Love Yourself

The Zero's Journey

We cannot change anything unless we accept it.
Condemnation does not liberate, it oppresses.
Carl Jung (8)

For the past thirty-five years, I have been involved in the sport of bodybuilding in one form or another: training myself in over 100 gyms, training others, competing, judging shows and promoting shows. As such, I have witnessed, over and over again, a rather curious phenomenon. There are lots and lots and lots of people of both sexes with magazine-level, quality physiques that absolutely loathe themselves! Furthermore, in my chiropractic practice, I have been privy to numerous patients who underwent gastric bypass surgery, lost tremendous amounts of weight and still "saw" a fat person staring back at them from the mirror every day! If you don't love who you are already, changing the "package" that your container is will not change that.

Our greatest enemies, the ones we
must fight most often, are within.
Thomas Paine (9)

Loving yourself must become a perpetual, genuine, full appreciation for who you currently are, who you were that led to who you currently are and then who you wish to become. Keeping in mind again that "God created man in His own image," you are reflections of Divinity. (10) Not

Weathering Accidental Enlightenment

loving yourself, as you already are, is criticizing the work of God! God doesn't need you to believe in Him. God *"is"* with or without your belief. God wants you to believe in yourselves! Trying to improve yourself without first believing in yourself will cause you to self-sabotage even the best of plans. If you feel unworthy, you will never allow yourself success.

Love yourself first and everything else falls into line.
Lucille Ball (11)

Years ago, while watching an episode of VH-1 Behind The Music, this concept really came together for me. Meatloaf, who I am a huge fan of, was being interviewed and he was discussing the cataclysmic loss of his voice following the colossal success of his first album, <u>Bat Out of Hell</u>. After years of loss and anguish, during a therapy session, Meatloaf finally found the cause of his strife. He told his therapist, "People are calling me a star and I don't like it!" (12) Once the problem was identified, correcting it was relatively simple. Meatloaf had to start thinking of himself and speaking of himself as a star. Positive affirmation, said over and over and over, until he believed it. Don't get me wrong, coming to a point of actually believing himself was not likely an easy task, but it was a relatively simple fix nonetheless. The bottom line is this, you will NEVER let yourself accomplish something that you don't feel you deserve, not for very long at least.

Remember those lists you made during the "Know Yourself" section? Go back to those now, particularly the lists of your perceived weaknesses and flaws. Your task now, should you decide to accept it (you do want positive change, right?!?) is to fall in love with everything on that list right now. Remember, everything on there is a reflection of God. Now, spend the time and effort necessary to fully appreciate the individuation of God in man that is you!

If you are feeling stuck in this section, here is a little trick to help you. Make a list of all of the traits you dislike or hate in others and start there. What you most dislike in others is often the mirrored reflection of what you have yet to accept in yourself. It keeps showing up to annoy you because what you resist persists and grows stronger, hence the strong negative emotions felt around it.

Improve Yourself

The first step toward change is acceptance. Once you accept yourself, you open the door to change. That's all you have to do. Change is not something you do, it's something you allow.
Wil Garcia (13)

Weathering Accidental Enlightenment

Now that you know yourself, your strengths, weaknesses, talents, passions and limitless capacity and now that you love yourself, fully appreciating the good, the bad and the ugly, you are in a position to successfully improve yourself, if you so desire. At the risk of sounding like Rodney Dangerfield's economics professor from the comedy film <u>Back To School</u>, essential, sequential step 3 from the 3-step process, Improve Yourself, consists of three sub-steps of its own. (14) To avoid further confusion, we will refer to them as steps 3A, 3B and 3C. So, without further ado:

- o **Step 3A:** Decide "What" [tangibles]

- o **Step 3B:** Up-level "How" [intangibles]

- o **Step 3C:** Act "as if" [strategies]

If you have read <u>iContractor 1... Constructing Your Perfect Life by Remodeling YOU from the Inside-Out!</u>, then you will likely recognize sub-steps 3A, 3B and 3C as the Always Believe In Your Dreams Coaching (SM) methodology. (15) For those of you not familiar with it, a brief review is in order.

Decide "What" [the tangibles]

> *Give me a stock clerk with a goal and I'll give you a man who will make history. Give me a man with no goals and I'll give you a stock clerk.*
> **J.C. Penney (16)**

What *do* you want? You can't expect to hit your target without first having a target to aim at. Decide up front, in advance, **exactly** what it is you wish to accomplish. Be able to describe it in exquisite detail. Put it in writing and give it a deadline. How much and by when? Don't get bogged down with questions about how it will come to be. Pick your target and take aim.

> *The greater danger for most of us lies not in setting our aim too high and falling short; but in setting our aim too low, and achieving our mark.*
> **Michelangelo (17)**

Most people invest more time into putting together a grocery list or planning out a vacation than they do deciding how they want their life to look six months, one year, five years, ten years into the future. Put the time and effort into it that your life deserves and do it right.

Up-level "How" [the intangibles]

> *One must not always think so much about what one should do, but rather what one should be.*
> **Meister Eckhart (18)**

Weathering Accidental Enlightenment

You will find that "HOW" you do what you do is infinitely more important than "WHAT" you actually do. Taking all of the right actions but with the wrong attitude of mind, will block you from accomplishing your desires. "HOW" you do "WHAT" you do sets the feeling tone.

Which feelings and emotions would be dominating your headspace if you had already succeeded? Would you be feeling more loving? More caring? More compassionate? More joyful? More giving? More grateful? How would you be? Is "HOW" you are currently being, on the inside, consistent with "WHAT" you are hoping to accomplish?

> *Who you are inside is what helps*
> *you make and do everything in life.*
> **Fred Rogers (19)**

Because life can only mirror back to you what you have previously put out there, the only way to create a better life is by creating a better image, a better "I am"-age to have life reflect back to you. Who will you need to become? What attitude of mind will you need to cultivate, adopt and emanate? By selectively choosing the thoughts you will think and the feelings/emotions you will express, you can take control of the direction your life is heading. Remember, success is an inside-out process that takes discipline, at least initially. What is the level of your commitment?

> *What we achieve inwardly will change outer reality.*
> **Plutarch (20)**

Act "as if" [the strategies]

> *Even when I was in the orphanage, when I was roaming the street trying to find enough to eat, even then I thought of myself as the greatest actor in the world.*
> **Charlie Chaplin (21)**

At a visceral, gut-feeling level, you already know what success looks and feels like to you. Consider your attitudes of being: how you would walk, talk, feel and be if you were already successful. This is not about creating something new. Rather, it is about allowing yourself to experience right now what you already possess inside of you. In other words, be **now** HOW you want to be when you are successful and you will be successful **now**!

There are a number of strategies you can employ to create the feeling of, the recognition of, already having it now. "Making room in your life for your dreams by making room for your dreams in your life" is one such strategy. (22) Practicing "right speech" so that the story you tell others

Weathering Accidental Enlightenment

about yourself actually supports your highest aspirations is another.

In his landmark book <u>The Success Principles</u>, Jack Canfield talks about how he attended a "come as you will be" party back in 1991 where all attendees were encouraged to show up "how they will be" once they have realized all of their dreams. (23) No details were to be left out. From manner of arrival to attire to topics of speech, they were to carry themselves, 100% in character, how they would if their dreams were already their current reality. Props were encouraged such as business cards, books they had written, awards they had received and magazine covers they had been featured on. I would recommend taking this one step further and striving to live every day as a "come as you will be" party.

Engage in activities now that create the feeling of having your dreams already accomplished. Find ways to awaken to the fact that you have already arrived. You are already there!

Steps and More Steps – Summary

Summarizing the essential, sequential, 3-step process:

1. Know Yourself

2. Love Yourself

3. Improve Yourself

Then, summarizing the 3 sub-steps:

> 3a. Decide "WHAT" – [tangibles]
> WHAT does your ideal dream life look like?
>
> 3b. Up-level "HOW" – [intangibles]
> HOW does your ideal dream life *feel*?
> Who must you *become* on the inside?
>
> 3c. Act "as if" – [strategies]
> Create the feeling of HOW to manifest the WHAT.

Weathering Accidental Enlightenment

Chapter 3

Finding Your AFFLATUS... Constructing Your Magnificent "Why"

Af ♦ fla ♦ tus - noun

(A) inspiration; an impelling mental force acting from within
(B) Divine communication of knowledge (1)

"Afflatus" is one of the sweetest sounding, most powerfully transformative words I have ever encountered in my lifetime. Derived from the classic Latin, and sometimes spelled 'adflatus' ["ad" (to) + "flatus" (blowing/breathing)], it is found in the ancient works of Cicero, as well as Horace and Virgil, and is used in the figurative sense to refer primarily to the "inspiration" or "breathing in" of the Divine Spirit. (2) This Divine Spirit "fills and overwhelms" a person and originates from the "animating breath of God (as) described in Genesis." (3)

Weathering Accidental Enlightenment

I first came across the word "afflatus" quite by serendipitous accident while researching either the correct spelling or meaning of some other since forgotten word. Never before or since have I come across a word with such far reaching importance. Your afflatus is your primary "raison d'être," your very reason for being!

Your innermost dreams and longings are not the result of random chance or circumstance. They exist within your soul because they have been Divinely communicated to you from God; they are YOUR afflatus, impelling you from within. iContractor 1 says, "Your dreams are your gifts from God. Following those dreams is your gift to God." (4) We are guided by Matthew 6:21 which states, "for where your treasure is, there your heart will be also." (5) Proverbs 17:8 says, "A present is a precious stone in the eyes of its possessor; wherever he turns, he prospers." (6) Proverbs 18:16 continues, "A man's gift makes room for him and brings him before great men." (7) However, 1 Timothy 4:14 cautions us, "Do not neglect the gift that is in you." (8)

Dreams are necessary to life.
Anaïs Nin (9)

Florence Scovel Shinn, a prominent "new thought" author in the early 1900s said, "there is a place that you are to fill and no one else can fill, something you are to do, which no one else can do;" something she referred to as your "Divine Design." (10) More recently, Viktor Frankl stated, "Everyone has his own specific vocation or mission in life to carry out a concrete assignment which demands fulfillment." (11) Paulo Coelho, author of The Alchemist, referred to it as "your Personal Legend... your mission on Earth." (12) In the Pixar classic Wall-E, his love interest, a robot on a mission to look for green plant life on planet earth, refers to her afflatus as her "Prime Directive." (13) Perhaps Vincent van Gogh summed it up best when he stated, "Your profession is not what brings home your paycheck. Your profession is what you were put on earth to do with such passion and such intensity that it becomes spiritual in calling." (14)

Finding your afflatus is not necessarily about having the job with the greatest income and acclaim. Neither is it about fighting the big battle or overcoming the big struggle or obstacle. Rather, finding your afflatus is about finding or creating your own "magnificent why." It's about allowing your soul to sing its song of jubilation and gratitude. It's about making use of the "gifts" given to you by God.

Russell Conwell, author of Acres of Diamonds and the founder of Temple University

Weathering Accidental Enlightenment

states, "We ought to teach that, however humble a man's station may be, if he does his full duty in that place, he is as much entitled to the American people's honor as is the king upon his throne." (15) Similarly, Martin Luther King, Jr. says, "If a man is called to be a streetsweeper, he should sweep streets even as Michelangelo painted, or Beethoven composed music or Shakespeare wrote poetry. He should sweep streets so well that all the hosts of heaven and earth will pause to say, here lived a great streetsweeper who did his job well." (16) Even the sacred Hindu text, The Bhagavad-Gita, says that it is "Better to do one's own duty imperfectly than to do another man's well." (17)

How important is it that we find, and then follow, our afflatus? Kahlil Gibran says, in The Prophet, "Work is love made visible. And if you cannot work with love but only with distaste, it is better that you should leave your work and sit at the gate of the temple and take alms of those who work with joy." (18) Proverbs 17:22 states, " a broken spirit dries the bones." (19) And Langston Hughes concurs when he says, "Hold fast to dreams, for if dreams die, life is a broken-winged bird that cannot fly." (20) As told in iContractor 1, "Your dreams are not just for you! They are meant to be expressed and increased for the good of us all." (21)

So, if finding and following your afflatus is so monumentally important, how come so few of us ever do it? Probably because it involves, at least initially, a lot of hard work! Arthur Jones, the inventive genius behind the Nautilus brand of weight training machines, says, "Human nature being what it is – and in my opinion, not being subject to much (if anything) in the way of large scale improvement – most people are not really interested in 'the truth' especially when it leads to unavoidably 'hard' solutions to their problems." (22) More than that, it involves scary work. Finding and following your afflatus requires that you quiet the voices of doubt in your mind and, instead, listen to the wee small voice within your soul. It requires that you learn to ignore the naysayers and societal pressures for conformity and, instead, each travel your own path ALONE. Ralph Waldo Trine states, "The great trouble with us is that we do not listen to and do not follow this voice within our own souls, and so we become as a house divided against itself." (23)

Along this solo journey, your faith gets severely tested. Saint John of the Cross referred to this spiritual crisis as "the Dark Night of the Soul," which he wrote about in 1578. (24) During this soul crisis, or "sole" crisis, if you will, as my wife calls it, with no end in sight and the odds seemingly stacked ever more against you, it is

Weathering Accidental Enlightenment

commonplace to just give up. In fact, most do! I would estimate that 50% or more of the population does not even bother to try following their afflatus; 40% may try half-heartedly but then they quickly give up at the first sign of difficulty; 8% will try **very** hard but still never make it through the "Dark Nights;" and only 1-2% will actually hang on until they succeed. These last two groups, the 8% and the 1-2%, are the ones who buy books, attend seminars and truly make an effort. These last two groups are you! [see Illustrations at end of chapter] Paulo Coelho writes, in <u>The Alchemist</u>, "the desert tests all men: it challenges every step, and kills those who become distracted." (25)

And in the luck of night
In secret places where no other spied
I went without my sight
Without a light to guide
Except the heart that lit me from inside.
Saint John of the Cross
(Excerpt from The Dark Night of the Soul poem) **(26)**

Tenacity pays off for those who do not give up, however. In <u>Think And Grow Rich</u>, Napoleon Hill states, "More than five hundred of the most successful men this country has ever known told the author their greatest success came just one step *beyond* the point at which defeat had overtaken them." (27) Speaking of his own journey to enlightenment, Lama Surya Das states, "I learned something that millions of seekers had also learned before me and millions will after me: you have to go through the darkness to truly know the light." (28) As my wise, "old soul" - young son tells us, "Some people stay in the dark so long that when they finally see the light, it scares them." (29)

Those who do not bother to try, or only try half-heartedly, do not necessarily fare any easier. Suppressed hopes and dreams have a way of making themselves known. (Appendix C explains some of the potential negative, dis-ease producing physiological consequences of not following one's afflatus.) Afflatus denied cries out ever louder until it can no longer be ignored. In an old episode of the <u>Fat Albert</u> cartoon, Bill Cosby said, "It's too bad that some of us have to be hit by lightning to get out of the dark." (30)

If I may, I would like to offer up an example of someone who was so hard-headed that he had to be "hit by lightning" multiple times before getting out of the dark himself; someone who bought a lifetime membership to painful experiences before he changed his ways. That someone is me! As anyone who has read <u>iContractor 1</u> or heard me speak knows, I have the prior track record of having gone broke 3x in 4 years before turning my life around; during the 2nd

Weathering Accidental Enlightenment

episode, I nearly died and during the 3rd episode, I came perilously close to homelessness.

> *Sometimes, it takes a painful experience*
> *to make us change our ways.*
> **Bible (31)**

This particular example focuses on my 2nd episode:

"In May of 2001, I found myself on the fourth floor of Meadville Medical Center, hovering between life and death following a ruptured appendix, peritonitis, septicemia and the associated emergency surgeries. Barely alive, unable to move or communicate and connected to life support, I felt as though my whole world had been ripped out from underneath me. This couldn't have just happened to me; I exercised regularly and watched what I ate. In fact, I had just trained down for a natural bodybuilding show! Angry and scared, knowing this would mean the closing of my office: Bright Spot Chiropractic, I was consumed by feelings of hopelessness.

> *He who has a why to live for*
> *can bear with almost any how.*
> **Friedrich Nietzsche (32)**

After my breathing tube was removed, I had been instructed to take short walks to re-build my strength and clear my lungs. But, movement was so painfully difficult and required such a mental psych-up period prior, that I wasn't really interested in participating! Then, one day, an angel of a nurse (one of the many wonderful healthcare workers who cared for me) by the name of Barbara, took my forearms into her hands, looked me in the eyes and said to me "Do you want to live or don't you?!? Then you have to get up and walk!" Then and there, I made the decision to live! What's more, I remembered how, prior to my illness, I had promised my six year old son that I would accompany him on his kindergarten field trip to the Erie Zoo; a field trip that would take place four short weeks following my life-saving surgery.

Empowered by my new sense of purpose and specifically wanting to keep my original promise to my son, rolling I-V stand and all, I went walking! After nine days, I was sent home to finish my recovery, open five-inch abdominal incision and all. Never did I take my eyes off of my goal, walking a little further every day. Two and a half weeks later, I made it! Even though my incision was still nearly two weeks away from full closure, I was able to keep my promise." (33)

The most precious gifts in life come hidden inside of painful wrapping paper.
Jacob Nordby (34)

Weathering Accidental Enlightenment

My turnaround, if you will, began when I made the decision to live. My decision to keep the promise I had previously made to my son became my "magnificent WHY" and empowered me to keep going through what was a long and painful recovery. As I grew stronger, both physically and mentally, I became more willing to listen to and ultimately, to follow, my own afflatus. I won't lie to you and tell you it happened overnight; it didn't. And, I won't pretend it was easy either. It took a lot of work before I became completely at peace within myself; getting to know AND love myself exactly as I am. I will tell you, though, it was absolutely worth it! If you are having trouble finding your afflatus, start by living your life passionately. When you live your life with passion, often your passion, your afflatus, finds you!

Consider for a moment great sculptors like Michelangelo, Rodin and Donatello. Sculptors don't add anything new to the blocks of granite or wood that they work with. Sculptors merely remove the extraneous "debris" to reveal the work of art that they already knew was in there. In any given block of granite or wood, there are an infinite number of potential masterpieces present. However, only through the vision and painstakingly hard work of the sculptor can the masterpiece be brought to life. Your afflatus is already inside of you too! All you have to do is uncover and honor it; strip away the extraneous patterns, personas and limits that have accumulated from society, upbringing and self-doubt.

If you find yourself in "lack" in any way, you are not yet "finished" or "polished;" you are still unaware of who you really are. To the unaware, an uncarved block of granite would appear to be without the work of art that is within it. That is certainly what would reflect back from a mirror if you were to look at it prior to chiseling away the debris. Likewise, if you are still cloaked in fear and self-doubt, your inner abundance will not be able to be reflected back to you. When Mark 11:24 states, "Whatever you ask for in prayer, believe that you have received it, and it will be yours," it is not suggesting this as a means to "trick" God into granting your heart's desire. (35) Rather, it is trying to wake you up to your true nature and your infinite abundance. Unfortunately, as George Bernard Shaw says, "Most people do not pray; they only beg." (36) As Luke 17:21 states so succinctly, "the kingdom of God is within you." (37) Tap into it NOW and claim your rightful heritage!

Death is not the enemy, living in constant fear is.
Norman Cousins (38)

Weathering Accidental Enlightenment

It does not matter how old you are or where you find yourself right now in life. Oliver Wendell Holmes says, "The greatest tragedy in America is not the destruction of our natural resources, though that tragedy is great. The truly great tragedy is the destruction of our human resources by our failure to fully utilize our abilities, which means that most men and women go to their graves with their music still in them" (39) Your music, your afflatus, has not gone away. It's still inside each and every one of you. If you listen to the melody of your soul, it will not lead you astray. Now is just as good a time as any to find and follow your afflatus. In fact, NOW is the only time you've got!

Time stays long enough for those who use it.
Leonardo da Vinci (40)

Any treatise on finding and following your afflatus would not be complete without considering the following eight areas of influence on such a journey. These eight areas are as follows:
- Attitude
- Faith
- Financial Consciousness
- Laughter
- Allowing
- Thanksgiving
- U.S.P. – Unique Selling Proposition
- Service

Chapters 4 through 11 will investigate each area of influence in more detail. And, while each of these chapters will contribute to the whole of your understanding, they have each been written so that they can stand alone as well.

Weathering Accidental Enlightenment

Following Your Afflatus

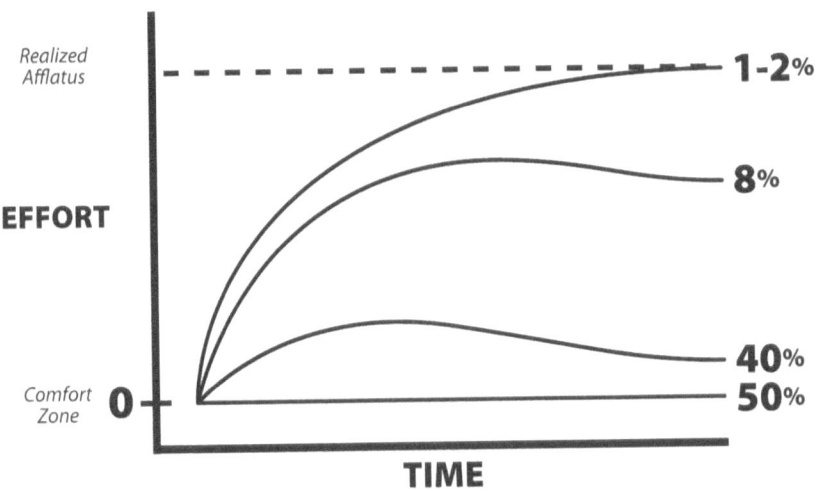

- **50%** - Don't bother to try

- **40%** - Try half-heartedly and quickly give up

Book Readers & Seminar Attendees {
- **8%** - Try very hard but never make it through the Dark Nights

- **1-2%** - Succeed

Chapter 4

AFFLATUS

Attitude

That which does not kill me makes me stronger.
Friedrich Nietzsche (1)

Giant Sequoia redwood trees in California are considered by some to be the largest living things on earth due to their incredible height, measuring over three hundred feet tall, and their incredible width, measuring up to twenty feet in diameter. There are some that are estimated to be more than three thousand years old. Part of their longevity stems from the fact that their bark can grow to be as much as four feet in thickness; an attribute which helps to make them fire resistant. Forest fires actually benefit them by wiping out the smaller trees that would otherwise compete for resources and eventually take over. (2)

In the heart of the Arabian Gulf, in the Bahrain Desert, there sits a lone tree, named the Tree of Life, which is estimated to be four to five hundred years old. This is particularly significant when one considers that the average life expectancy for this type of tree, a mesquite tree

Weathering Accidental Enlightenment

from the Acacia family, is typically only one hundred years under the best of conditions. This particular tree has managed to survive the harsh desert climate by sending roots hundreds of feet deep to where they can be fed by a natural spring. (3)

In the woods where I live, there are literally hundreds, of thousands of trees; some tall, some stout, some bent and gnarled, others thin and spindly. When my family and I first moved to the woods, I used to go out following heavy snow storms, of which we have many, and knock the heavy, wet snow from the bent, encumbered limbs. Then, one day it dawned on me that I was actually putting these trees at greater risk by not allowing them to strengthen on their own. As I gazed at the biggest, strongest and most magnificent trees in our forest, I came to realize each bend, twist and disfigurement as a testament to the obstacles each tree had overcome; a witness to the inner strength that carried certain trees forward on their perpetual journey to touch the sky.

Much like the trees, every one of you, if you live long enough, will eventually experience hardship and loss on some level. When this happens, you will be faced with two choices: you can either let it **define and destroy** you OR you can use it to **strengthen and empower** you; you can either let yourself become hardened and closed by bitterness or you can become softened and opened *with loving compassion*. You get to choose via your response. Those of you who allow each and every obstacle and hardship to define and destroy you will suffer the effects from a self-imposed imprisonment by the thoughts and feelings/emotions that you have chosen: blame-by-blame, justification-by-justification, excuse-by-excuse, complaint-by-complaint. But know this, you are your own jailer! When you let hardship of any kind define you, it's all you think about, it's all you talk about, it's what you become about and eventually, it is going to take you out!

> *Your living is determined not so much by what*
> *life brings to you as by the attitude you bring*
> *to life; not so much by what happens to you*
> *as by the way your mind looks at what happens.*
> **Kahlil Gibran (4)**

Most people do not choose illness, hardship and lack, at least not overtly. Indirectly, by default, through the thoughts you previously have thought, the feelings/emotions that you have previously allowed yourself to express and through the actions you have previously taken, or neglected to take, you may have, at least, contributed on some level. However, this is not about "blaming the victim," so to speak. Think

Weathering Accidental Enlightenment

more in terms of "response-*ability*" instead of responsibility. Regardless of the situation or circumstance you now find yourself faced with, you can choose your next response. The ONE thing, which is the ONLY thing, you have any real control over is your ATTITUDE OF MIND… and that is the ONLY thing you need to change in order to change EVERYTHING!

> *To different minds, the same world*
> *is a hell, and a heaven.*
> **Ralph Waldo Emerson (5)**

During a televised episode of Oprah's "Lifeclass" featuring guest, Pastor Joel Osteen, Oprah referenced motivational speaker Tony Robbins whom she said says that most people think that life happens "to" them when, in actuality, life happens "for" them. (6) I would like to add the following clarifications: for people with a "victim-mentality," life does appear to happen "to" them; for people with a "victor-mentality," who feel that they create their own reality, life appears to happen "from" them. However, in both instances, I would say that life happens "for" them If AND ONLY IF, no matter what happens, they **choose** to look for the benefit and thereby make it "for" them. Every situation has good and bad, positive and negative. Where you **choose** to place your focus is what makes all of the difference. Viktor Frankl, a survivor of four WWII concentration camps of the Holocaust, called it "the last of the human freedoms – to choose one's attitude in any given set of circumstances." (7)

It all really boils down to one thing: FAITH. Viktor Frankl also says, "Just as a small fire is extinguished by the storm whereas a large fire is enhanced by it – likewise a weak faith is weakened by predicament and catastrophes whereas a strong faith is strengthened by them." (8) Fear creates resistance. Fear is nothing more than faith in a negative outcome; backwards faith, if you will. F.E.A.R., to me, says to "Forget Everything And Run!" The very reason stepping into your fear, acting in spite of fear, is potentially so powerful of an exercise is because it can demonstrate your faith, ultimately, in a positive outcome; in your ultimate victory. It can be the antithesis of running away. However, when evaluating any possible action steps to be taken, the real litmus test for which ones are most acceptable hinges on the underlying motive behind your actions: are they based in fear or are they based in faith? Are you running away from something or towards something? Are these action steps moving you further away from or closer to your dreams? What really is your underlying attitude of mind when engaging in your action steps?

Weathering Accidental Enlightenment

I think the most important decision we make is whether we believe we live in a friendly or hostile universe.
Albert Einstein (9)

Letting go of resistance requires that you have more faith than fear; that you come to believe that whatever happens is in your best interest; that you come to believe that the universe (God) really does support you in every way. It does not mean that you give up or don't care any more. Rather, it means that you trust that the outcome will be in your favor; you have faith in the outcome. There is good and bad in every situation and circumstance. You get to choose your thoughts and feelings/emotions (attitude of mind). By focusing always and only on the positive, no matter what happens to or around you, it *will* always be "for" you, containing positive elements. Knowing this and fully owning it allows you to approach life with a child-like, anticipatory excitement: "What good thing(s) will present themselves to me next?"

Faith and belief are ALL about carrying yourself and behaving in a manner where there is not a shred of evidence to support your views. So is insanity. Enjoy the ride! Learn to look for and expect the positives in every situation always. Carry yourself with an attitude of mind that says, "no matter what happens, it will contain elements that benefit me." Go out into the world expecting

The Zero's Journey

to be fully supported in your dreams and give thanks both for the ride and for already having arrived!

God asks no man whether he will accept life. This is not the choice. You must take it. The only question is how.
Rev. Henry Ward Beecher (10)

Weathering Accidental Enlightenment

Chapter 5

aFflatus

Faith

Faith is spiritualized imagination.
Rev. Henry Ward Beecher (1)

Faith, a word bandied about by so very many divergent groups and organizations, each seeking to promote or validate their own cause or agenda, yet understood by so very few individuals; a word charged with emotion and meaning yet so difficult to comprehend. And, if you don't fully grasp it's meaning, how can you ever hope to properly apply it and unleash it's power to do good within your own lives? How can you tap into its power to realize your own afflatus?

Perhaps it will be helpful to first clarify all of the things that faith is not. Contrary to popular usage, faith is not the title for any particular religious sect or organization. Neither is faith a means to "appease" some deity. As mentioned in Chapter 2, God doesn't need you to believe in Him. God/Source/Universe "is" with or without your belief in Their existence. Faith is not a public affirmation or display made to garner acceptance

Weathering Accidental Enlightenment

by your peers. Neither is it mere agreement with someone else's words, mine included. Faith is not evident when we engage in incongruency between what we think, feel, say and do. Faith is lacking in the farmer who, as Earl Shoaff says, digs up his seeds to see if they are growing yet. Mr. Shoaff, who was Jim Rohn's original mentor, taught that true showings of "Lack of Faith" present themselves when we overly concern ourselves with finding detailed answers to questions about our dream fulfillment such as, "I wonder where it's coming from?," "I wonder when it's coming?" and "I wonder how it's coming?" (2) Trying to "force" outcomes is definitely not an act of faith. Getting "lost at SEE," as my wife calls it; in other words, "I'll believe it when I see it!" is not an act of faith either.

> *Faith is to believe what we do not see; the reward of this faith is to see what we believe.*
> **Saint Augustine (3)**

In the Bible, Hebrews 11:1 states, "Faith is the substance of things hoped for, the evidence of things not seen." (4) Faith is an overwhelming belief in self; a "burning desire," as Napoleon Hill calls it, in the expectation of accomplishing your aim. (5) Faith is an unrelenting journey through the "Dark Night of the Soul" that refuses to concede defeat, refuses to succumb to the "night terrors" and refuses to give up. Faith is not having a "back-up" plan, not having a "plan B." Sun Tzu, in the 2400 year old classic text <u>The Art of War</u>, says, "Throw the troops into a position from which there is no escape and even when faced with death, they will not flee. For if prepared to die, what can they not achieve?... In a desperate situation they fear nothing; where there is no way out they stand firm." (6) He continues, with respect to good leaders, "He burns his boats and smashes his cooking pots... cuts off their return route just as if he were removing a ladder from beneath them." (7) "Throw them into a perilous situation and they survive... For when the army is placed in such a situation it can snatch victory from defeat." (8) Faith is 100% commitment; it's not partial and it's not casual.

Faith is...

    Knowing that you know that you know!

Faith is...

    Unshakable

    Unbreakable

    Unmistakable

    Non-forsakable

    Rouses the unwakable

Weathering Accidental Enlightenment

Bottom line: You ARE able!

Faith is…

Unfailing

Not bailing

Despite all the railing

No matter how far trailing

And through all the wailing…

Knowing you will prevail!!!

Examples of people with unshakable faith are easy to find in the history books. They are the movers and the shakers; the leaders who have changed the course of history time and time again. People such as South African President Nelson Mandela, a man who spent twenty-seven years confined to a prison cell because of his outspoken views about apartheid; a man who ultimately succeeded and went on to be elected to his country's highest office. Another example can be found in His Holiness the 14th Dalai Lama, spiritual Tibetan leader whose Tibetan government has been in exile since 1959 when he fled to India after the People's Republic of China asserted control over Tibet. Viktor Frankl, survivor of four

The Zero's Journey

WWII concentration camps of the Holocaust, is another. Even after being captured by the Nazis and having his life's work, his manuscript, burned before him, he never gave up the hope that one day he would be released, publish his manuscript, which he carefully re-wrote on scraps of trash, and re-build his practice and speaking career; all of which did come to pass! And Mother Teresa, whom we will talk more about in the next chapter, is another fine example of someone who lived their life through faith.

Good faith is its own reward.
Lao Tzu (9)

Wilma Rudolph, the first woman in the world to win three gold medals in track and field during a single Olympic games, and considered to be the fastest woman in the world during the 1960s, is another stellar example of someone who developed an unshakable faith. Born prematurely and sickly as a child, she was struck with infantile paralysis, caused by the polio virus, at the age of four. By the age of eleven, Wilma had suffered through polio and scarlet fever. (10) But, in Wilma's own words, "My doctors told me I would never walk again. My mother told me I would. I believed my mother." (11) Her faith continued to grow to where she could finally say, "I believe in me more than anything in this world." (12) Even Muhammad Ali has been quoted as saying, "I am

Weathering Accidental Enlightenment

the greatest; I said that even before I knew I was." (13)

A champion is someone who gets up when he can't.
Jack Dempsey
Heavyweight Boxing Champion of the World (14)

As mentioned in chapter three, everybody gets their faith tested while pursuing their dreams. Nobody is immune from "the Dark Night of the Soul," no matter what the level of their previous accomplishments; not even me. A curious phenomenon often times occurs when you commit yourself 100% to your afflatus: before your afflatus shows any signs of life whatsoever, EVERYTHING else seems to go South! Whether this is the Universe's way of fully testing your resolve, a means of "making room for your dreams in your life" as suggested in iContractor 1 or just a result of loss of focus on your older, prior dreams, I cannot say with any certainty. (15) But, it has happened to enough fellow travelers, as well as to myself, to see it as a formidable force to be reckoned with. When I wrote the manuscript for iContractor 1, my chiropractic practice, Ketcham Chiropractic, PLLC, was rocking! While publishing iContractor 1 and working to lay the foundation for my Always Believe In Your Dreams, LLC business, however, my patient volume decreased by approximately one third; a loss it never recovered from. During the writing of

The "Zero's Journey" (this book, originally titled iContractor 2.0), and while working to get my public speaking and writing careers off the ground, patient volume decreased yet again by a similar amount. This time, however, due to simultaneous, statewide insurance industry changes, per-visit reimbursement levels also declined by nearly 50%. Thus, by the time this book was approximately half written (this chapter actually!), and still without any paid speaking venues lined up, and next to no book sales of iContractor 1, I, the one with the track record for having gone broke 3X in 4 years over a decade ago, again found myself in the precarious predicament of being broke yet once more! With revenues running at less than 25% of what they used to be, I found my faith severely tested. Only the strength of my faith, fueled by the burning passion and clarity of my vision were likely to see me through. When Christmas came along, with no money in the bank whatsoever, way behind on bills and seemingly no light at the end of the proverbial tunnel, even my wife, my first and longest running fan, questioned my sanity and struggled with great difficulty to maintain any semblance of hope for a better tomorrow; any faith whatsoever in me to deliver it! Admittedly, as both of our properties (chiropractic office and home) went into foreclosure in early January, things did appear to be hopelessly lost.

Weathering Accidental Enlightenment

Anthony Robbins says, "You're in the midst of a war, a battle between the limits of a crowd seeking the surrender of your dreams, and the power of your true vision to create and contribute. It is a fight between those who will tell you what you cannot do, and that part of you that knows, and has always known, that we are more than our environment, and that a dream, backed by an unrelenting will to attain it, is truly a reality with an imminent arrival." (16)

> *Life is a fight for territory and once you stop fighting for what you want, what you don't want will automatically take over.*
> **Stephen Duncanson**
> [quoting Dr. Edwin Louis Cole, deceased founder of The Christian Men's Network] (17)

One of life's harshest lessons is coming to terms with the fact that you must perpetually fight for all that you hold dear if you want to make it through successfully. It does not matter who you are or what you have accomplished previously, you must NEVER give up fighting for everything you desire to be, do and have; for everything you desire to achieve. In fact, in the very moment you want to give up, that is when you must give it all you've got. That is when you are on the brink of your biggest breakthroughs.

Where do we look to strengthen our faith? Buddhist teacher, Sister Ayya Khema, states,

"What we are looking for lies within us, and if we gave our time and energy to an interior search, we would come across it much faster, since that is the only place where it is to be found." (18) She continues, "We all have the answers within ourselves, we just have not gotten in touch with them yet. The potential of finding the truth within requires faith in ourselves." (19)

Everything in the Universe is
within you. Ask all from yourself.
Rumi (20)

Faith requires that you persist through the darkness where you cannot see, with nothing more to illumine your path or soothe your troubled soul than the belief that, as long as you continue to show up, always being and doing your very best, better days lie ahead for you. If you can accomplish this one task, you will have succeeded where most others have failed! As II Corinthians 5:7 reminds us, "For we walk by faith, not by sight." (21)

I will restore to you the years that the swarming locust
hath eaten... You shall eat in plenty and be satisfied.
Bible (22)

Weathering Accidental Enlightenment

Chapter 6

AFFLATUS

Financial Consciousness

He is much to be dreaded who stands in dread of poverty.
Publilius Syrus (1)

In and of itself, money is innocuous and benign. You give meaning to it through the attitudes of mind that you view it with. You can infuse money with love and positivity, seeing it as a means to animate your dreams. Likewise, you can infuse money with hate and negativity; blaming it for all that is wrong in the world. Some point to the Bible as their "proof" that "money is the root of all evil." However, 1 Timothy 6:10 states clearly that "the *love of* money is the root of all evil." (2) Russell Conwell, in Acres of Diamonds explains, "The man that worships the dollar instead of thinking of the purposes for which it ought to be used, the man who idolizes simply money, the miser that hoards his money in the cellar, or hides it in his stocking, or refuses to invest it where it will do the world good, that man who hugs the dollar until the eagle squeals has in him the root of all evil." (3)

Weathering Accidental Enlightenment

Money is analogous to air and the flow of money is a lot like breathing. As you inspire, or breathe inward, money comes into you as income and as you expire, or breathe outward, money flows out as expense. You live in a world with an abundance of air that allows you to breathe in AND out naturally, normally and with ease. Constricting or constipating the natural flow, either in or out, would cause you discomfort and dis-ease. When you breathe in, you don't typically take in extra gulps of air just in case the well runs dry, so to speak. You breathe in just what you need, knowing all of your breathing needs will continue to be met. Likewise, when you breathe out, you don't hold some air back in case of suffocation. You just breathe out fully **knowing** that there will be more air available to you to breathe in when you need it. There is no thought given to shortage or lack. And yet, with regard to money, most people behave VERY differently. Psalm 23 states, "I shalt not want... my cup runneth over." (4) That passage is not meant to apply to some arenas but not others. If we truly come from abundance, then ALL of our needs have **already** been met.

Your wealth is too near to you.
You are looking right over it.
Russell H. Conwell (5)

Hard to fathom as this may be, Mother Teresa lived her whole ministry in accordance with this principle, never keeping any reserves of money on hand. "Her method of fund-raising was to pray... God had always provided what she needed, never more, never less... She operated more than 400 centers in 102 countries, and they **always** seemed to have exactly what they needed." (6) Can you imagine successfully managing a multimillion-dollar business with no cash reserves? That is a testament to the strength of her faith; something we can all aspire to!

Money is a tool that, much like breathable air, is vital for life. It is not to be hoarded. Neither is it to be hated. It is to be used to animate, to give life to, your afflatus. Now, you may be thinking to yourself, "If money is like air, why does it feel like I am suffocating?"

> *Teach me, O God, not to torture myself, not to make a martyr out of myself through stifling reflection, but rather teach me to breathe deeply in faith.*
> **Søren Kierkegaard (7)**

Part of the problem stems from our inclination to "chase our pennies" rather than "chasing our passions." Often times, we are tempted to quit our jobs and/or change careers in our attempts to raise our pay. If your sole goal is to increase your income, the first thing you need to

Weathering Accidental Enlightenment

do is to up-level your financial consciousness. And to do that, you need to become a new you on the inside because, for success, you don't need to go SOMEWHERE else, you just need to *become* SOMEONE else.

Before quitting your job or changing careers for something "new," you have to ask yourself if you would be happy in your new vocation even if you only made the exact same amount as you are currently making. After all, you are the same you on the inside, with the same financial consciousness. Going one step further, what if you changed jobs or careers and you actually made less money? Ask yourself, "Would I be willing to do _____ (fill in the blank) as a career, even if I had to do it for free?" That's a good way to see if you are really only "chasing pennies" or if you are truly "chasing passions." Oftentimes, in the pursuit of a "new" direction, your buried consciousness patterns or blueprints regarding money can become magnified and more evident. Only the strength of your afflatus will get you through those "dark nights." Penny chasers won't make it!

> *Can anybody remember when the times were not hard and money not scarce?*
> **Ralph Waldo Emerson (8)**

There are a whole host of reasons to consider a change in career such as: following your dreams, new interest, the chance for greater stimulation, increased level of contribution or impact. However, by itself, a change in income is not likely to be sufficient to fulfill and sustain you. And, a word of caution, if you are chasing virtually any career because it looks "glamorous" to you, you are likely to be looking at it through the blinders of infatuation; what I refer to as "infatuation blinders" or "lala goggles."

Going back to school for further training can also be a great way to improve yourself and your situation. But, it can also serve as a distraction from dealing with your real issues, like your financial consciousness. And, those issues will demand your full attention sooner or later. Sometimes too, this can seem like a "safer" way for someone to follow their afflatus by way of a long, circuitous journey. For instance, I knew of a colleague, when I was in chiropractic school, who was going to school to become a chiropractor so that he could then amass enough money to someday open an import business; his true afflatus. This is not as uncommon as you might think. I recently encountered another young woman who is making preparations to attend pharmacy school so she can become a pharmacist and then amass enough money and credibility to

Weathering Accidental Enlightenment

become an author, speaker and lifestyle coach. In both instances, in my humble opinion, they could have taken all of the time, effort and money and just used them to pursue their real interest in the first place.

> *This time, like all times, is a very good one, if we but know what to do with it.*
> **Ralph Waldo Emerson (9)**

Wealth, in and of itself, is a consciousness. It is a recognition AND acceptance, an allowing, of all of the abundance that already is. Part of becoming prosperous and wealthy centers on coming to a recognition that you both *have* "enough" and *are* "enough" already and then being grateful for all you have. When Bright Spot Chiropractic closed, I was so focused on all that I thought I was lacking at the time that I didn't leave room to appreciate all of the abundance and prosperity that was still there. My family, my wife and two small children, still loved and cared for me dearly. My father was still living at the time as well. And, all of them were healthy. My health had taken quite a blow, but at least I was still alive too! What's more, I still had food in my fridge, clothes on my back, a roof over my head and a safe place to sleep; which according to an anonymous saying I have encountered numerous times since, made me richer than 75% of the rest of the world. What I eventually came to realize was, while I have been financially broke or bankrupt many times, I have NEVER lacked for abundance, prosperity and wealth regardless of whether I recognized and acknowledged such at the time.

As I came to understand, however, it is important to recognize and acknowledge your abundance sooner than not. Matthew 25:29 states, "For everyone who has will be given more, and he will have an abundance. Whoever does not have, even what he has will be taken from him." (10) Similarly, Luke 19:26 says, "To everyone who has, more will be given, but as for the one who has nothing, even what he has will be taken away." (11)

The man who is content with what he has is not in danger of loss.
Lao Tzu (12)

Dr. John Demartini, acclaimed author, speaker and chiropractor, talks about the need for you to "declare what you're worth." (13) This comes down to a self-worth issue. Remember "Know Yourself" and "Love Yourself" from Chapter 2? Don't expect anyone else to recognize and acknowledge the value of what you do, or who you are, until you yourself recognize and acknowledge it first. Learn to declare your worth, demand it and expect it!

Weathering Accidental Enlightenment

Motivational consultant to NASA and Olympic athletes, Denis Waitley, has an interesting philosophy when it comes to money. He says, "If you chase money, it may catch you — and if it catches you, you'll forever be its slave. By letting money pursue you, but never catch you, you'll always be its master." (14) What he is referring to is doing more than expected, going the extra mile in everything you do. This is **not** about denying your worth. Rather, this is about declaring your worth; the worth of your services, for instance, and then delivering a level of service that far exceeds even that! Consider this, when you buy something of great value, like a house, a car, fine jewelry and such, you tend to appreciate your purchase even more if you got a particularly good deal on it, whether in terms of price, rarity, etc. But, if you "pay through the nose" for it, you don't typically appreciate it as much and you may even grow to resent it. It does not matter how much something actually cost you IF you feel that you got a particularly good deal on it. Over-deliver on all of your promises and you will forever be in demand and amply compensated!

If you see yourself as prosperous, you will be. If you see yourself as continually hard up, that is exactly what you will be.
Robert Collier (15)

The Zero's Journey

Give without restraint and just breathe, knowing full well that all you need will be there for you when you need it!

Weathering Accidental Enlightenment

Chapter 7

AFFLATUS

Laughter

Laugh my friend, for laughter ignites a fire within the pit of your belly and awakens your being.
Pilar Stella & Cynthia Aliza Blake (1)

When we are very young, our lives literally overflow with dreams, joy and laughter. By some estimates, most four year olds laugh as much as five hundred times a day! As we grow older, and for many, as their dreams become a distant memory, laughter becomes a very rare commodity indeed. Yet, it is important to remember that life is far too weighty of a matter to be handled without a sense of levity.

The most wasted day of all is that on which we have not laughed.
Sébastien Roch Nicolas Chamfort (2)

The benefits of laughter, both mental and physiological, are many and well documented. An entire field of study, known as gelotology, has emerged to study the effects of laughter on the body. Physiologically, laughter has been shown to stimulate circulation, increase heart rate, stabilize blood pressure, massage internal organs, facilitate digestion and elimination, increase oxygen supply to muscles, decrease muscle tension, stimulate the immune system, decrease stress hormones such as cortisol and epinephrine, release endorphins and promote an overall sense of well-being. Norman Cousins, author of <u>Anatomy of an Illness</u>, which documents his recovery from the debilitating effects of rheumatoid arthritis through the use of high-dosage, intra-venous Vitamin C supplementation combined with laughter therapy, writes, "Ten minutes of genuine belly laughter had an anesthetic effect and would give me at least two hours of pain-free sleep." (3) Five minutes of belly laughter has been equated to three minutes of strenuous cardiovascular exercise. And Zen Buddhists believe that fifteen minutes of laughter equates to six to eight hours of meditation.

> *We don't laugh because we're happy,*
> *we are happy because we laugh.*
> **William James (4)**

Perhaps, for our purposes here, laughter's biggest selling point rests in its ability to moderate unpleasant situations and accompany you as you journey through "the Dark Night of the Soul" on the path to following your afflatus. Viktor Frankl, survivor of four WWII concentration camps of the Holocaust, reports, "I never would have made it if I could not have laughed. It lifted me momentarily out of this horrible situation, just enough to make it livable." (5) Charlie Chaplin adds, "To truly laugh, you must be able to take your pain and play with it." (6) Because, as Mark Twain reminds us, "Against the assault of laughter, nothing can stand." (7)

> *God is a comedian playing to*
> *an audience too afraid to laugh.*
> **Voltaire (8)**

Maintaining your sense of humor, particularly as you journey through "the Dark Night of the Soul," enables you to reclaim a modicum of control over your emotions, control over your response to the circumstances of your life. And, as you choose your responses, you better situate yourself to enjoy the process as you follow the path to your own afflatus.

> *Do not take life too seriously.*
> *You will never get out of it alive.*
> **Elbert Hubbard (9)**

Just as the monsters in Pixar's classic film, Monster's Inc., found to be true, laughter is much, much, much more powerful than screams to fuel your life! (10)

Weathering Accidental Enlightenment

Chapter 8

AFFL**A**TUS

Allowing

*The longer we dwell on our misfortunes,
the greater is their power to harm us.*
Voltaire (1)

When following your afflatus, it is normal to want to try to micro-manage everything; to try to "force" outcomes that are not developing fast enough, fully enough, to satisfy your demands. Unfortunately, this actually blocks your dreams from coming true at all. Viktor Frankl states, "Ironically enough, in the same way that fear brings to pass what one is afraid of, likewise a forced intention makes impossible what one forcibly wishes;" something he termed "hyper-intention." (2) The very act of trying to "force" an outcome says that you do NOT have faith in God/Source/Universe to answer your prayers and fulfill your desires. This "hyper-intention," this tendency to try to "force" outcomes, is typically the end result of your resistance to what "is" combined with your struggles to see a light at the end of the tunnel; a glimmer of luminescence in "the Dark Night of the Soul." However, when you

Weathering Accidental Enlightenment

make the decision to believe in a friendly Universe, to believe that God knows what He is doing, that He really is on your side and always has been, then you can stop resisting what is happening. At that point, you are able to stop struggling and raging against all that has already taken place and cannot be altered in any way anyways.

Once you have set your intentions by "Deciding WHAT" you want and you have "Up-leveled HOW" by improving your attitude of mind and you have begun to "Act 'as if'" to train your eyes to "SEE" your abundance, it is essential that you "ALLOW" your afflatus to unfold in its own time, in its own way. You don't give up or cease to care. Rather, you demonstrate FAITH; you TRUST that God/Source/Universe really does love and support you in every way: whatever happens really is in your best interest; your best interest is truly being looked out for and served at all times!

Sometimes, it can be difficult to differentiate between "allowing" and "giving up." Imagine that you are piloting a powerful spacecraft through time and space as you journey towards your afflatus. "Allowing" means setting your trip co-ordinates and then engaging the cruise control mechanism whereas "giving up" means crash landing your spacecraft and parking it

forever. "Allowing" involves a gentle steering, nudging with desire, whereas "giving up" involves moving from a white-knuckle level of forced control to nothing. "Allowing" is based in TRUST and FAITH whereas "giving up" is based in hopelessness, apathy and despondence. More than anything else, "allowing" is about letting go of your attachments; attachments to:
- Things
- People
- Money
- Goals/dreams
- Outcomes

"Allowing" is about expressing your desires WITHOUT making rigid attachments to their fulfillment.

> *You have to take it as it happens, but you should try to make it happen the way you want to take it.*
> *- Old German Proverb (3)*

Most people spend excessive amounts of time and energy fighting what "is" and trying to "force" outcomes whose time has not yet arrived. When you give up this one-sided fight and endless struggle with yourself, you free up countless resources that you can more productively use in the present moment. Being "present in the moment," as Eckhart Tolle writes so eloquently about in <u>The Power of Now</u>, enables you to see all

Weathering Accidental Enlightenment

of the abundance that is already yours; it enables you to be in gratitude now. (4) And, being in gratitude now changes the feeling tone you are emitting, which in turn will up-level what gets reflected back to you via the Law of Reflection.

Crystalize your vision, take steps, however small, every day in the direction of your dreams, always doing your very best, and then ALLOW the Universe to dazzle and amaze you as it selects the best vectors and timing.

In iContractor 1, we made use of a "train analogy" to explain the differing roles played by your thoughts, feelings and actions when constructing your perfect life and following your afflatus. A review of the train analogy is in order here:

"Your thoughts, feelings and actions all play a role. But, your feelings set the overall tone. Think of your feelings as the train track that sets your course. Your thoughts and actions serve as the fuel cells for the train engine. Positive or negative feelings determine where the track is headed. Your thoughts and actions serve as the fuel cells made either of coal (if they are in alignment with your feelings) or of water (if they are in opposition to your feelings). The one can power the train engine, really ramping up its power and speed. The other douses the fire and slows the engine to a crawl, sometimes even stopping it cold. But, only the direction of the tracks (your feelings) determines your ultimate destination." (5) [see Illustrations that follow]

"Consistency and congruency are the keys. Consider them 'the C & C of success!'" (6)

Building upon this train analogy, ALLOWING means TRUSTING that train tracks exist at all to take you from where you are, Point A, to where you want to go, Point B. ALLOWING also necessitates having FAITH that the specific track you are currently on actually leads to your desired destination. ALLOWING does not mean trying to lay the track down while your train is in motion. Hanging from the front of the train engine, frantically laying down track where you think it should be, all the while squeezing the life out of the engine controls, is definitely not ALLOWING. Your strong DESIRE is what determines which train you actually board. After getting on board, how your train of Desire, the "C & C Express," gets from Point A to Point B is none of your concern! Don't spoil the trip by trying to wrestle the controls from the engineer (God/Source/Universe).

For after all, the best thing one can do when it is raining is to let it rain.
Henry Wadsworth Longfellow (7)

Weathering Accidental Enlightenment

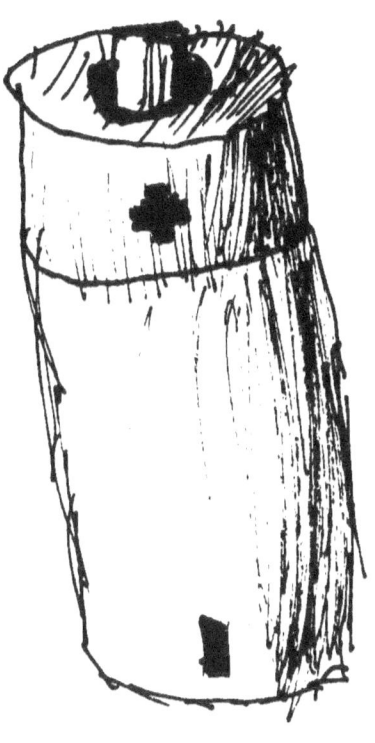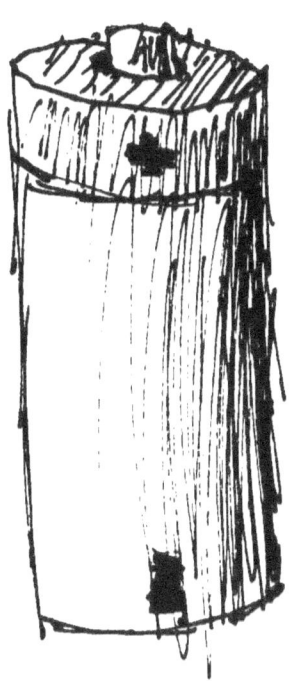

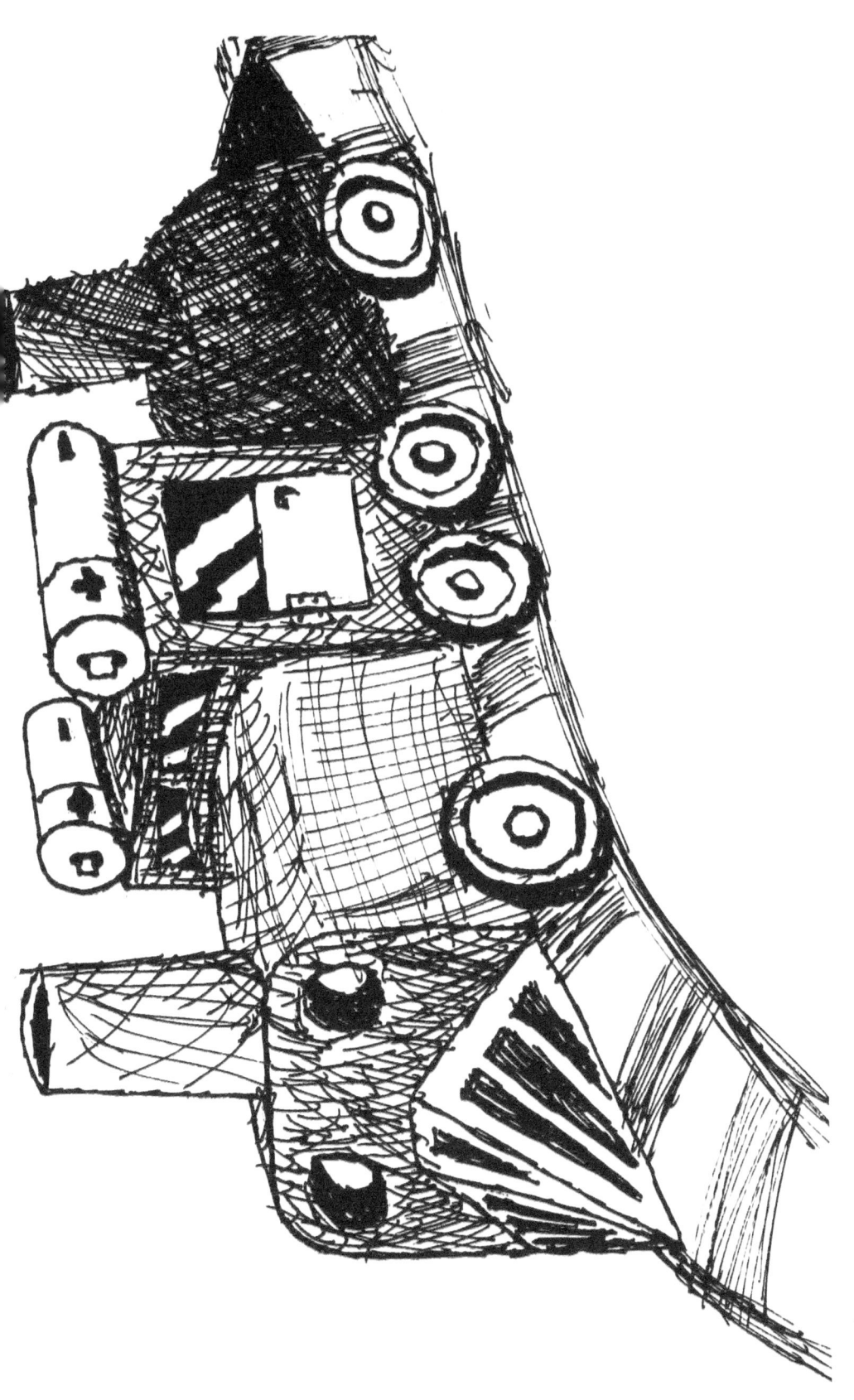

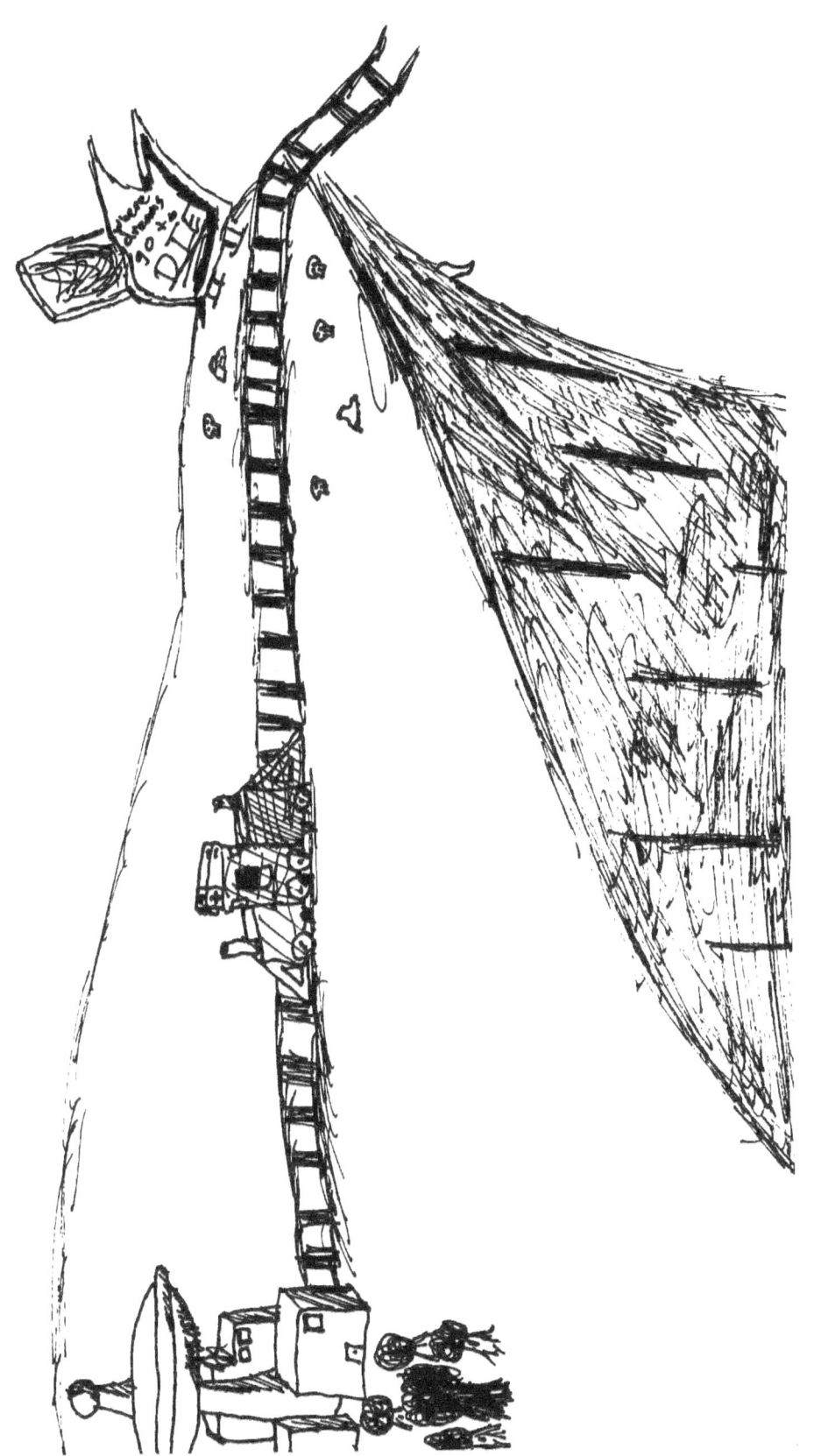

Chapter 9

AFFLATUS

Thanksgiving

Practically the whole human race is hypnotized, thinking whatever it is told to think.
Ernest Holmes (1)

According to George Bernard Shaw, "Two percent of the people think, three percent of the people think they think, and ninety-five percent of the people would rather die than think." (2) Bertrand Russell concurs when he states, "Most people would rather die than think; in fact they do so." (3) More often than not, most people are not thinking at all. They are not following their afflatus. They are just looking for a group of people standing in line somewhere so that they can join with them without regard for where the line is heading, without regard for whose afflatus they are actually furthering. Finding and following your afflatus mandates that you step out of line and learn to think for yourself from here forward. What's more, you will reach your destination far sooner if you will learn to frame your thoughts in the many hues of gratitude.

Weathering Accidental Enlightenment

He that is down, needs fear no fall.
John Bunyan (4)

No matter where you currently find yourself, no matter what the nature of your current circumstances, you can *always* find something to be grateful for. In fact, before you expend any more energy looking to your future or lamenting about your past, you would do well to give focused time and effort to finding elements in your present circumstances to be thankful about. Resisting what "is" and lamenting what "isn't" causes you to completely miss out on the magic of the moment.

There is a beautiful wall plaque hanging in my house, from an anonymous author, which states, "Contentment is not the fulfillment of what you want, but the realization of how much you already have." Find gratitude in your heart for *all* that you already have, for *all* that you have persevered through and for who you have *already* become. Unpleasant experiences are not to be resented or forgotten. Just like the pressure that creates the diamond from a lump of coal and the friction that polishes the finest rubies, your trials and tribulations have forged you into who you are today. Be thankful for their role in polishing your luster.

Once you can be at peace with your past and your present, and truly thankful for how they have contributed to the masterpiece-in-progress that is you, then you can add thankfulness for who you are becoming and who you will soon be. As discussed earlier, giving thanks in advance is a VERY powerful exercise, not as a means to "trick" God/Source/Universe into giving you your "stuff" but as a means of recognizing and acknowledging all that *already* is! This is about coming to an inner knowing and acceptance, a FAITH and ALLOWING, of the abundance that is *already* yours. Your "stuff" will show up when you truly and fully recognize and acknowledge that you were never without it in the first place!

Give light, and the darkness will disappear of itself.
Desiderius Erasmus (5)

Giving thanks is not a one-time event; it is not a seasonal event either. Thanksgiving is a way of life: a twenty-four hours a day, seven days a week, perpetual way of being. In the Bible, 1 Thessalonians 5:18-19 says to, "Render constant thanks... Do not put out the Spirit's fire." (6) Henry Ward Beecher, unaware of the Law of Reflection, stated, "The unthankful heart... discovers no mercies, but let the thankful heart sweep through the day and, as the magnet finds the iron, so it will find, in every hour, some heavenly blessings!" (7)

There are always flowers for those who want to see them.
Henri Matisse (8)

Weathering Accidental Enlightenment

Chapter 10

AFFLAT**U**S

U.S.P. "Unique Selling Proposition"

Learn to... be what you are, and learn to resign with a good grace all that you are not.
Henri Frederic Amiel (1)

In biology, molting is a process whereby an animal such as a snake will shed their old skin once it gets too tight for them. As it outgrows its old skin, a snake will be compelled to rub its head against rough surfaces, causing the already stretched skin to split and peel backwards on itself, similar to taking your socks off inside-out, until the snake can then crawl out entirely. This process repeats on a regular basis as the snake continues to mature and grow. (2) Should the snake fail to successfully shed its old skin, however, it perishes. How many of you could honestly profess to being comfortable in your own skin? Judging from the surging popularity of cosmetic surgeries, weight-loss supplements, extreme exercise programs and the like, I would venture to say that it is very few indeed!

Weathering Accidental Enlightenment

In light of my thirty-five plus years of involvement with bodybuilding, people are often shocked to learn just how little importance I give to the external condition of a person's state of being. But, the truth of the matter is that I work out with weights because I love lifting weights and really for no other reason. Physiques are the true "shape-shifters" as evidenced by the rapidity with which a person's physical development is erased by a single illness or injury. Yet, hopefully, whom they have recognized and developed themselves to be on the inside is completely impervious to such calamity.

To be nobody but yourself in a world which is doing its best night and day to make you like everybody else means to fight the hardest battle any human being can fight and never stop fighting.
e.e. cummings (3)

Now, please don't tell the nutrition Nazis, the fitness fanatics and the Surgeon General, but I personally would much rather take the risk of living a shorter life while being true to myself, true to who I was created to be, than to increase my potential lifespan by forever struggling to become someone I am not. I recognize that mine is not the mainstream opinion and that this is controversial territory, especially in today's climate of "ideal" body type, focus on BMI (Body Mass Index) and recent attempts by insurance companies and the pharmaceutical industry to "police" blood chemistry numbers such as cholesterol. Far better, in my opinion, to love yourself for who you already are than to perpetually loathe yourself for who you are not. You can still change and "improve" yourself if you so desire. But the real starting point has to be from a place of total acceptance, already loving yourself for who you were uniquely created to be.

> *Someone's opinion of you does*
> *not have to become your reality.*
> **Les Brown (4)**

So many of us live our lives based around worrying about what other people will think of us. But, according to Dr. Daniel Amen, psychologist and author of <u>Change Your Brain, Change Your Life</u>, they may not be thinking of you as much as you like to think! (5) Dr. Amen refers to what he calls the "18/40/60 Rule" which goes as follows: at age 18, you worry about what everybody thinks of you; at age 40, you don't care what anybody thinks of you; at age 60, you realize that nobody was thinking that much of you anyways! (6)

In other words (mine, actually), during Stage I (age 18), we are seeking approval from others. We are wanting to comply and conform to the wishes and expectations of others. During Stage II (age 40), we begin to live our lives in defiance of the wishes and expectations of others.

Weathering Accidental Enlightenment

We rebel. Finally, during Stage III (age 60), we begin to live our lives solely for ourselves. This is not a selfish stage; rather, it is about finally being true to who we are. Recognizing our own mortality, we begin to take our lives off of hold and listen to our own inner longings.

While the "18/40/60 Rule" is a good "rule of thumb," many never make it past Stage II (age 40). In fact, some don't even make it past Stage I (age 18). There is an old African proverb that states, "If there's no enemy within, the enemy outside can do you no harm." (7) Who would/could you be if you made the shift TODAY to Stage III?!? Who are you really? Do you even really know?

Part of the problem stems from our academic system itself. We spend inordinate amounts of time studying the knowledge and opinions of others but little to no time getting to know ourselves. George Addair, author of <u>In Search Of The Invisible Forces</u> and founder of The Omega Vector and The Delta Vector, states, "Millions of young college grads think they are ready for life when they are more out of touch with themselves than when they were freshmen. They lost themselves in school." (8) He continues, "Without self-knowledge, life is an impossible dream." (9) This has certainly been true in my life. When I was a freshman in college at Saint

The Zero's Journey

Bonaventure University, back in the early '80s, I was much more together and sure of myself than I was four years later at graduation. In fact, I would venture so far as to say that it has taken me the ensuing thirty years to get myself back to where I was when I started!

> *Don't surrender your individuality... if you do ... you become a slave and the chances are that in time you will be unable to hold even the respect of those whom you in this way try to please.*
> **Ralph Waldo Trine (10)**

You see, when I was a freshman, I was content being the non-conformist that I was. I had never really "fit in," so to speak, and that was perfectly alright with me. But, as I continued on through my schooling, the pressure to conform to an "acceptable" model increased exponentially. Even while studying chiropractic at Palmer College of Chiropractic, a profession founded and developed by rugged individualists, the pressure to conform was ever increasingly present. In his acclaimed chiropractic text <u>Are You The Doctor, Doctor? The Philosophy Of Successful Practice</u>, Dr. Fred Barge states, "Like it or not, those who would seek the success, the acclaim, prestige and esteem of the doctor, must fit into the mold. Uncomfortable as it may seem at first, any attempt not to comply will certainly stand in the way of early professional success." (11) In spite of my best efforts to comply, it was to no avail. After

Weathering Accidental Enlightenment

going broke three times in four years while complying and force-fitting myself in to the acceptable mold, I found myself completely lost and unsure of who I was at all!

Emerson states, "It is easy in the world to live after the world's opinion; it is easy in solitude to live after our own; but the great man is he who in the midst of the crowd keeps with perfect sweetness the independence of solitude." (12) Most people fail, in my humble opinion, not because of their non-conformist tendencies, but rather due to their efforts to conform. By attempting to "fit in," they suppress their true nature. If you know yourself and truly love yourself, how could you possibly deny that?!?

> *If God had wanted me otherwise,*
> *He would have created me otherwise.*
> **Johann Wolfgang von Goethe (13)**

What is your U.S.P.? Find out what makes you you; identify it, celebrate it, maximize it and live fully into it! Be who God uniquely created you to be. As my good friend and fellow author **Jacob Nordby** says: **"Blessed Are The Weird People... poets, misfits, writers, mystics, heretics, painters and troubadours... for they teach us to see the world through different eyes." (14)**

The Zero's Journey

Weathering Accidental Enlightenment

Chapter 11

AFFLATUS

Service

*No one is useless in this world who
lightens the burden of it for anyone else.*
Charles Dickens (1)

Most people are searching for relevance in their daily lives, a sense of meaning, some way of affirming that their existence actually matters in the lives of others. As promoted in both the Parable of the Talents and the Parable of the Minas, at the core of our being, most of us want to utilize the gifts that we have been endowed with. (2,3) As we live into our afflatus, most of us realize that our gifts were never intended solely for us, to be hoarded and kept hidden. We want to help others. We realize that, as we help others, we really help ourselves. Wilfred Grenfell takes it one step further by reminding us, "The service we render others is the rent we pay for our room on earth." (4) Thus, as Herman Melville states, "We cannot live only for ourselves. A thousand fibers connect us with our fellow men." (5) In other words, Life isn't just about YOU, it never was; it's about us, ALL OF US TOGETHER!

Weathering Accidental Enlightenment

Our prime purpose in this life is to help others and if you can't help them, at least don't hurt them.
Dalai Lama (6)

It is not likely that it will be easy, but it will be worthwhile. As Nietzsche reminds us, "Life always gets harder toward the summit-the cold increases, responsibility increases." (7) That responsibility is to your fellow man. In the words of Henry David Thoreau, "All men want, not something to *do with*, but something to *do*, or rather something to *be*." (8) Be of service!

If you want to pay homage to the reflection of Divinity that is within you, then it is imperative that you find your afflatus, follow your afflatus and then live into who God created you uniquely to be. Tap into your Divinity and then share it with others. Find your own light and then use it to illuminate the path for others who are still struggling to find their way out of the darkness!

Johann Wolfgang von Goethe says, "Treat a man as he is and he will remain as he is. Treat a man as he can and should be, and he will become as he can and should be." (9) Perhaps this is the highest and noblest use of the Law of Reflection. As discussed in Chapter 1, whatever we emit is what gets reflected back to us. Likewise, we reflect back to others whatever they have emitted.

The Zero's Journey

However, we can override our "reflective" tendency by *intentionally choosing* to recognize the Divinity within others, even those who are not yet aware of it within themselves, and reflect that back to them instead! In doing so, by loving the unlovable, we give others, perhaps for the first time in their lives, glimpses of their own Divinity, their own true nature, and enable them to live in to it thus up-leveling all of humanity.

This has certainly played out in my lifetime. In Chapter 3, I told the "story" of my appendix episode and how one nurse in particular, Barbara, got me back in to the game of life. Yes, I was very fortunate having such a wonderful surgeon and team of healthcare workers to save my physical container. But Barbara gets ALL of the credit for picking up the shattered pieces of my spirit and putting them back together again. By seeing more in me than I was able to see in myself, by loving me when I was anything but lovable, she accomplished what "all of the king's horses and all of the king's men" could not. (10)

You have not lived today until you have done something for someone who can never repay you.
John Bunyan (11)

Thanks to Barbara, not only did I get to be there for my son on his kindergarten field trip, as I had promised him I would, but I got to be there for

Weathering Accidental Enlightenment

ALL of both of my children's major events: field trips, concerts, talent shows, recitals, illnesses, birthdays, holidays, EVERYTHING for the past thirteen years!

We may never know the far reaching impact of the things we think, say or do today. But know this, by *intentionally choosing* to recognize the Divinity in others, we are saving lives every day!!! I can think of no greater service to humankind than this!

What do we live for if not to make
life less difficult for each other?
George Eliot (12)

Chapter 12

Walking in Silence — Solitary Refinement

When you pray, rather let your heart be without words than your words without heart.
John Bunyan (1)

Now that you have investigated each of the eight areas of influence (Chapters 4 through 11) on your journey to finding and following your afflatus, it is necessary to consider the realm of prayer in order to bring it all together. But first, so that everyone is on the same page, let's define "prayer."

Prayer, as I have come to understand it, can be defined as ANY interior exercise or journey that serves to connect you with your own Divinity. It is the means by which you can relate to and interact with God/Source/Universe. It is the means by which you awaken to and remember who you really are. Prayer can also be divided into two very different approaches: meditative prayer and contemplative prayer. Meditative prayer is the approach most people are familiar with and it is also the approach most in use by Western religions today, even though Christianity included and promoted contemplative prayer in earlier times.

Weathering Accidental Enlightenment

Meditative prayer consists primarily of telling, begging and striving. It is an "active" modality whereby you are attempting to influence or control particular future outcomes. Here, you are pushing your own agenda, "doing" something. There are two basic forms of meditative prayer. The first is rote recitation, where you memorize and regurgitate the words of others. The second form of meditative prayer is reflection, where you utilize affirmations and visualization along with active thinking. Essentially, meditative prayer consists of "Transmission" of your desires to God/Source/Universe. And, while meditative prayer is good for getting clear about your desires, Saint John of the Cross considered it to be the realm of "beginners" to spiritual practice.

And when you pray, do not keep on babbling... (for they think they will be heard because of their many words)... your Father knows what you need before you ask Him.
Bible (2)

Contemplative prayer, on the other hand, consists of listening and allowing. It is a "passive" modality whereby you are primarily getting conditions ready so that God/Source/Universe can contact you; "being" a certain way. Efforts are more focused upon "letting go and letting God," as they say; upon letting go of your attachments. Here, you are accepting of a higher purpose;

accepting of the will of God/Source/Universe. In this instance, "connection" to this higher power is not something you can "push" into existence. Rather, when it comes, it comes as a gift. Contemplative prayer is mostly silent, as you stay focused on the present moment; on "what is." Essentially, contemplative prayer is about "Reception" and acknowledges that God/Source/Universe already knows your desires. Saint John of the Cross considered contemplative prayer to be the domain of the "progressives."

Making the shift from meditative prayer to contemplative prayer, from telling to listening, from striving to allowing, from controlling to accepting, is sometimes a voluntary choice. However, as you will find out in the next couple of chapters, sometimes it evolves as more of a necessity, a coping mechanism or survival strategy, so that you do not perish when circumstances around you do not cooperate right away with your plans.

> *We know that God makes all things work together for the good of those who have been called according to His decree.*
> [Personally interpreted to include:
> ...according to the following of your afflatus]
> **Bible (3)**

Weathering Accidental Enlightenment

Moving from "beginners" to "progressives," as Saint John of the Cross labels them, demands walking in FAITH; faith that God/Source/Universe really does love AND support you and your dreams/afflatus. During these times, "cosmic coincidences" and "serendipitous synchronicities" will become your lifelines, connecting you to something greater than yourself, tethering your sanity in the dark. After all, the overriding purpose and value of spirituality lies in encouraging and supporting your cooperation with the plans that God/Source/Universe already has for you and, in actuality, has already begun to initiate in your lives.

Do not say of anything,
"I will do that tomorrow,"
without adding, "God willing."
Quran (4)

Alexander Graham Bell states, "When one door closes, another opens, but we often look so long and so regretfully upon the closed door that we fail to see the one that has opened for us." (5) However, not all doors open the same way. There are times in life when you can PUSH through these unlocked doors of opportunity with ease: making plans, setting goals and making measurable progress. And then, there are times when PUSHING, slamming yourself against these doors that must be PULLED, only causes you to suffer bruising. Learning to recognize which doors to push and which doors to pull might quite possibly be the hardest lesson any of you will ever face.

Let us follow our destiny, ebb and flow. Whatever may happen, we master fortune by accepting it.
Virgil (6)

The move from a "meditative" existence to a more "contemplative" existence is often heralded by a Dark Night of the Spirit, which you will learn more about in great detail in the following chapter. In fact, this particular Dark Night is also sometimes called the Dark Contemplation. More often than not, you will be forced to question your own Divinity as you are graduated from an intellectual knowledge of God/Source/Universe to an actual, experiential understanding; an understanding that defies words and represents true enlightenment.

No faith is our own that we have not arduously won.
Havelock Ellis (7)

Weathering Accidental Enlightenment

Prayer Summary

Meditative Prayer
- Telling / begging / striving
- "Active" / controlling
- PUSH
- Rote recitation & Reflection
- Doing
- Transmission to
- Good for getting clear on your desires
- "Beginners"

Contemplative Prayer
- Listening / allowing
- "Passive" / accepting
- PULL
- Mostly silent
- Being
- Reception from
- God already knows your desires
- "Progressives"

Weathering Accidental Enlightenment

Chapter 13

Weathering the "Dark Nights" — A Tale of Two Survivors

In a real dark night of the soul it is always three o'clock in the morning.
F. Scott Fitzgerald (1)

Back in 1578, while imprisoned by his Carmelite brothers who opposed his reformations to their religious order, Saint John of the Cross wrote a landmark poem, <u>The Dark Night of the Soul</u>, which describes the journey of the soul from its physical, earthly home to its union, or re-union, with God or Source. (2) Subsequent to writing this poem, Saint John of the Cross then wrote a two-volume treatise to explain the meaning of it all. The "Darkness," according to Saint John, represents the hardships and difficulties the soul meets in detaching from the physical world and reaching for the light, the union with the Creator.

Saint John's treatise divides the Dark Night of the Soul into two distinct stages: the Dark Night of the Sense and the Dark Night of the Spirit. In both instances, what worked for you before no longer does and there is a sense of abandonment, a

Weathering Accidental Enlightenment

feeling that all spiritual blessing is over for you in this lifetime. As I understand and have experienced it, Stage I, the Dark Night of the Sense, results directly from what you are emitting. The consequences of your negative thinking and feeling are now being reflected back to you full force. Any inconsistency and incongruency of prior thoughts, feelings and actions also tends to show up here. Everybody experiences the Dark Night of the Sense during the course of their lifetime, some more frequently and more intensely than others. Essentially, you have done things in such a way, maybe with the best of intentions even, negatively just the same, that you now have negative consequences to deal with. A lot of people refer to the effects from this stage as Karma. The beauty of Stage I is that it gives you an opportunity to take 100% responsibility for your results thus far. If you have created something that is not to your liking, now you are presented with the chance to recognize your role and to create anew something more desirable. When I went broke 3X in 4 years (1999, 2001 and 2003), I was most likely in Stage I.

When the past no longer illuminates the future, the spirit walks in darkness.
Alexis de Tocqueville (3)

Stage II, the Dark Night of the Spirit, is the far less common and far more intense of the two stages. Unlike Stage I, this time you have done things positively, in a consistent and congruent manner; but, where are the fruits of your labor? This true crisis of faith is now brought on by the prolonged delay between all of your positive emissions of thought, feeling and action and their subsequent positive reflection back to you. This stage is marked by an anguishingly painful period of seeming "invisibility" where nothing seems to be happening for you, despite your best efforts. Viktor Frankl, in describing the life of a typical concentration camp member, coined the term "Provisional Existence of Unknown Limit." (4) He called this "the most depressing influence of all… it was impossible to foresee whether or when, if at all, this form of existence would end." (5) It is during this same period that a new level of consciousness is being birthed. Special care and attention must be given to resist the urge to abort your dreams or let them become stillborn at this time. "Response-*ability*" is crucial now. For the rest of this discussion, I will be dealing primarily with Stage II, the Dark Night of the Spirit.

There are a variety of life events that can trigger such a Dark Night. Sudden, drastic changes in:
- Health: illness (self or loved ones), breaking addictions

Weathering Accidental Enlightenment

- Relationships: marriage, divorce, death of a spouse or partner
- Family Structure: death of a parent or sibling, birth or death of a child
- Career: graduation, new job, loss of job
- Finances: bankruptcy, loss of business, market corrections, inheriting money
- Extended Stage I: lag between old results and new results can trigger Stage II

In all of the above instances, the anguish, pain and mental torment felt during the perceived long lag time between emitted desire/dream/afflatus and its reflected reality is both real and consequential. Hopelessness abounds and suffocates. Saint John of the Cross, in his interpretive tome, <u>Dark Night of the Soul</u>, describes it best saying, "What the sorrowful soul feels most in this condition is its clear perception, as it thinks, that God has abandoned it... When this purgative contemplation is most severe, the soul feels very keenly the shadow of death... and the pains of hell... All this is felt by the soul in this condition – yea, and more, for it believes that it is so with it forever. It feels, too, that all creatures have forsaken it... 'my friends and acquaintances, they have counted me an abomination'." (6)

Questions and uncertainties arise that threaten to shake the very foundational beliefs your entire life, thus far, has been built upon. This is where I found myself during the writing of <u>The "Zero's Journey"</u>. As mentioned in Chapter 5, FAITH, my particular crisis came on as a result of the massive (75%) decline in my chiropractic revenues while writing and striving to market myself as a motivational speaker. I had spent the past three years writing my books and newspaper articles, designing and building my website (AlwaysBelieveInYourDreams.com), developing my talks and creating a media presence. I had "Decided" very clearly WHAT I wanted my life to look like. I had done the internal work to "Up-level" such that HOW I was being on the inside was consistent with WHAT I was hoping to accomplish. And I had been Acting "as if," living into the picture of the life I so strongly desired. I had been utilizing visualization and positive affirmations consistently and congruently throughout this period. Yet, here I was now, faced with the very real possibility of losing everything tangible I had ever owned! I found myself with next to no resources, no prospects and no practical way to downsize.

Questions flooded my consciousness. "Will everything really be OK?" I questioned EVERYTHING! I questioned:

Weathering Accidental Enlightenment

Prior choices:

- "Should I have done _____ instead?"
- "What if I had done _____?"
- "Should I have stayed in accounting and never pursued my dream of becoming a chiropractor twenty-one years ago?"
- "Maybe I should have picked a different bachelor's degree thirty years ago, gotten my master's and taught at a University?"
- "Was I foolish to follow my heart? My dreams?"

Current direction:

- "Do I need to change direction now?"
- "Which direction should I go?"

Future possibilities:

- "Can I realistically accomplish my goals?"
- "What if I get another job instead? Does this mean I am giving up?"
- "Is this only a temporary set-back?"
- "Could this be a stepping stone to my dreams?"

Very existence:

- "Why was I born in the first place?"
- "Why am I still here?"
- "Does ANYTHING matter anymore?"
- "Am I dying?"
- "Am I really more valuable to my family dead than alive (due to life insurance proceeds)?"
- "Am I strong enough to survive this?"

A man may fulfill the object of his existence by asking a question he cannot answer, and attempting a task he cannot achieve.
Oliver Wendell Holmes (7)

These questions were made all the more serious by the many grave uncertainties I found swirling all around me:

- "Would I lose my house?"
- "Would I lose my weight room?"
- "Would I lose my office?"
- "Would I lose my personal library?"
- "Would I lose the apartment above my office where I stored all of my childhood memorabilia, including my deceased mother's ceramics from pre-1981?"
- "Would I be forced to get another job?"

Weathering Accidental Enlightenment

- "Would I be forced to go back to accounting to make ends meet? This would represent a double dream reversal!"
- "Would my wife, Lisa, live through this Dark Night?"
- "Would my marriage survive this Dark Night?"
- "Would I end up homeless? Widowed? Divorced?"
- "How would I ever provide for my family again?"
- "Would I ever get a paid speaking engagement?"
- "With all of the health issues I suffered following my ruptured appendix, would I be able to physically tolerate a forty plus hour work week?"
- "Would I have to quit practicing chiropractic altogether? If so, who would take care of the patients who had come to depend on me?"
- "Would I be able to continue working out?"
- "Would I survive my Dark Night?"
- "Who would I be without any of my stuff?"

The Dark Night of the Spirit is embodied in the Bible when Jesus cried out, while nailed to the cross, "My God, My God, why have You forsaken Me?" (8,9) Psalm 22:1 continues, "Why are You so far from helping Me, and from the words of My groaning?" (10)

Eckhart Tolle, commenting on the "Dark Night" says, "Really what has collapsed then is the whole conceptual framework for your life, the meaning that your mind had given it." (11) I love having and using all of my stuff *but* I am not my stuff. I AM with and without every last bit of it. Who I have become, or grown into, can NEVER be taken away from me *unless* I choose to surrender it myself! And therein lies the greatest risk contained within the Dark Night of the Spirit. Viktor Frankl writes with regard to daily prison life, "A man who let himself decline because he could not see any future goal found himself occupied with retrospective thoughts... But in robbing the present of its reality there lay a certain danger. It became easy to overlook the opportunities to make something positive of camp life, opportunities which really did exist... Life for such people became meaningless... The prisoner who had lost FAITH in the future – his future – was doomed." (12) In the Bible, Galatians 6:9 tells us, "Let us not become weary in doing good, for at the proper time we will reap a harvest if we do not give up." (13) James 1:12 concurs saying, "Blessed is the man who perseveres under trial, because when he has stood the test, he will receive the crown (victory wreath) of life that God has promised." (14)

> *One should be able to see things as hopeless and yet be determined to make them otherwise.*
> F. Scott Fitzgerald (15)

This brings me to my partner for the past 22 years, the love of my life, my wife Lisa. Apparently, Lisa and I really do think very much alike. Deciding to herself that she had more value to me deceased than alive (again, due to life insurance proceeds), she stopped eating and gave up completely half way through the month of January. While Lisa had no specific illness at the time, her actions were bound to have powerful, potentially grave consequences. Viktor Frankl notes, "Those who know how close the connection is between the state of mind of a man – his courage and hope, or lack of them – and the state of immunity of his body will understand that the sudden loss of hope and courage can have a deadly effect." (16) O. Carl Simonton, M.D. writes in Getting Well Again how, "Chronic stress results in a suppression of the immune system." (17) Dr. Simonton, a renowned oncologist, states, "Emotional and mental states play a significant role in susceptibility to disease, including cancer." He continues, "Cancer is often an indication of problems elsewhere in an individual's life… The cancer patient has typically responded to these problems and stresses with a deep sense of hopelessness, or 'giving-up'." (18) I had seen my own mother perish under similar circumstances when I was sixteen years of age. Elisabeth Kübler-Ross, M.D. writes, in her landmark work <u>On Death and Dying</u>, "If a patient stops expressing hope, it is usually a sign of imminent death." (19) And so, with everything else crumbling around me, it became necessary to also devise a plan to rescue my wife from the bowels of hell.

Fortunately for the both of us, the simple 3-step process I had created previously, the Always Believe In Your Dreams Coaching (SM) methodology, fit the bill perfectly:

Decide to stay!

First and foremost, Lisa had to make a decision, a commitment, to stay. After having given up completely for over a week, this was no small task. It required that she make a commitment to herself like she had never done before, like she would if she were making a commitment to a small child or a spouse. It required that she take the full intensity of her doubt and flip it, utilizing it to commit to seeing her decision through. Lisa had thrown everything about life and about herself in the trash. Flipping it would require her to muster absolutely everything she had left inside of her. This was what I asked from her for my birthday present and it was the biggest thing I have ever asked of anyone.

Up-level how you are feeling inside.

Next, I advised Lisa to count her blessings daily, hourly if need be. She needed to replace her feelings of terror with feelings of gratitude because the one cannot exist in the presence of the other. Now, more than ever, it was imperative that she find a way to interrupt the endless loop of worry, fear and self-doubt that kept playing itself over and over in her head.

Act "as if"

Finally, I taught Lisa to stay present in the current moment. Focus on the blessings and bounty in the current moment, the now. Yes, the reality was not pretty. We were in default on multiple credit cards. We had narrowly escaped two foreclosure proceedings on our properties, thanks to the magnanimous generosity of two of my good friends and Lisa's mother. The bank was continuing to treat us as lepers. We were dealing with court proceedings related to the credit cards. Nearly all of our subscriptions had lapsed and we had to return our satellite boxes, leaving us without any form of television. And, we had very little to no money on hand. Yet, we had plenty of food in our cupboards and food in our fridge. We had a working refrigerator and the electricity to power it. We had a warm, dry house. Even if we had been in foreclosure, in the current moment it was still ours! We had each other and that was far more than many we knew of. There was no danger in this minute. There was no danger in this hour. There was no danger in this day. I taught Lisa to not let her mind and emotions race away with worries about tomorrow. I helped her to focus on this day, this hour, this minute only. Don't look beyond anything you are not currently appreciative of. Being present in the current moment allowed her to step away from her fears, her "night terrors," even if only momentarily, so she could think clearly and tap into the feeling tone of her gratitude for all of the blessings she still had. In time, these momentary reprieves from the "night terrors" got longer and stronger and more productive. Being present in each moment enabled Lisa to get to where she could say "All is well," even if only for the current moment. Once she could say that, she could begin to act "as if" all is well in every moment. Acting "as if" all is well did not just reduce her stress in the current moment. It also enabled her to keep taking positive steps, however small those steps may

Weathering Accidental Enlightenment

have been, towards her dreams. I will not say it was easy for Lisa; it was not. Some days, staying present in the current moment was a minute-by-minute struggle that required repeated efforts at counting her blessings. But, in time, it got easier and more natural for her to do.

This same simple, 3-step process saw me through this painful period as well. Summarizing the 3 steps:

1.) Decide to stay and see things through:
- However *long* it takes
- *Wherever* it takes you to

2.) Up-level your internal state of being:
- Count your blessings REGULARLY!
- Every time you find yourself re-playing in your mind that non-stop track of worry, fear and self-doubt, interrupt it by counting your blessings. If you are going to obsess about something anyways, make it something positive.

3.) Act "as if" ALL IS WELL!
- Stay present in the current moment: minute-by-minute, hour-by-hour, day-by-day
- In the current moment, ALL IS WELL.
- Now, act "as if" all is well in *EVERY* moment!

- Try tapping into how you will feel when all works out in your favor in the future.
- Believe in yourself and your unlimited potential.
- Trust the process of life.
- Have FAITH in the outcome.
- Know that you are infinitely loved and supported.
- All is well now AND it will continue to be so in all future moments as well.

ALLOW everything to unfold as God/Source/Universe intends. Trust the process of life to unfold without unraveling. Allow the sands of time to run without you tonight! There is nothing to fear. Be thankful NOW! And, keep moving forward, maintaining your original focus.

Faith is the strength by which a shattered world shall emerge into the light.
Helen Keller (20)

Not everybody gets to experience the Dark Night of the Spirit. Painful though it is, the birthing of a new level of consciousness is truly a gift. Goethe says, "There is strong shadow where there is much light." (21) I firmly believe that, the closer you are to a true and full recognition of who you really are, the more likely you are to experience this. As you tap into your own

Weathering Accidental Enlightenment

Divinity, the brighter and less impeded your own light becomes, the greater the shadow it can cast! Australian novelist and playwright Morris West states, "One has to accept pain as a condition of existence. One has to court doubt and darkness as the cost of knowing. One needs a will stubborn in conflict, but apt always to the total acceptance of every consequence of living and dying." (22)

Every one of you will encounter adversity during the course of your lifetime, maybe even a Dark Night of the Spirit. But, you don't have to let it define you. Your life will be defined, ultimately, by the choices you make in responding to your own Dark Nights, by who you choose to be, moment-by-precious-moment. Choose in favor of YOU!!!

The depth of darkness to which you can descend
and still live is an exact measure of the
height to which you can aspire to reach.
Pliny the Elder (23)

Chapter 14

The Coming of the Dawn

One may not reach the dawn
save by the path of the night.
Kahlil Gibran (1)

I used to love to quote quantum physicist Niels Bohr who stated, "An expert is a person who has found out by his own painful experience all the mistakes that one can make in a very narrow field." (2) I would then, somewhat jokingly, follow that up by stating, "That's me!" Because I had "been there, bled that!", I truly thought that I had obtained "expert" status. (3)

But, if there is one thing I have learned from the Dark Night of the Soul, or more precisely, the Dark Night of the Spirit, it is this: The more I learn about everything, the less, I now realize, I know about anything! Journeying through the Dark Night of the Spirit has been a truly humbling experience. Letting go of my attachments and learning to release the stranglehold I had on all of my hopes and dreams so that I could ALLOW the process of life to unfold in its own time, in its own way, was incredibly awkward and excruciatingly painful. Coming to the realization that I was not in

Weathering Accidental Enlightenment

complete control, like I thought I was, was very frightening indeed.

> *For it is by grace you have been saved, through faith — and this not from yourselves, it is the gift of God — not by works, so that no one can boast.*
> **Bible (4)**

I am NOT an expert. In fact, it is highly unlikely that I will ever use the term "expert" again in reference to myself. I am just an ordinary guy, like every one of you, a fellow traveler of light who has read a lot and experienced a whole lot more. But, by no means do I have all of the answers.

Dr. Gerald May is the author of a modern book titled <u>The Dark Night of the Soul</u> which attempts to interpret Saint John of the Cross' original works by the same name. He states, "Maybe, sometimes, in the midst of things going terribly wrong, something is going just right." (5) Neale Donald Walsch, author of <u>Conversations with God</u>, concurs when he states, "I have learned to trust the *process* of life, and not so much the outcome. Destinations have not nearly as much value as journeys." (6)

> *The only certainty is that nothing is certain.*
> **Pliny the Elder (7)**

The Zero's Journey

The nature of life is change. And, the more we strive to keep things the same, the greater the changes seem to be. Nothing lasts forever. We only need to visit any cemetery to get a fresh reminder of the transient nature of our existence. Economies and industries rise and fall. Remember Kodak film? How about vinyl records, cassette tapes and VCRs? Even Chiropractic is not immune to change. It is a given that, at some point in time, in each one of our lives, we will all experience the bitter taste of failure as well as the savory sweetness of success; the vulnerability of weakness as well as the gift of inner strength; the fragility of illness as well as the radiance of health; the emptiness of abandonment as well as the nourishment of love; the paralyzing effects of fear as well as the faith-building effects of courage; the poverty of ignorance as well as the well-spring of new knowledge. Of course, we all hope to spend most of our days on the right-hand side of this equation, basking in abundant success, strength, health, love, courage and knowledge. However, the only guarantee in life is that NOTHING is guaranteed!

Sometimes, the best that we can hope for is to first learn to truly love ourselves, as we already are, and then to love everyone else, as we have learned to love ourselves. Perhaps that is the greatest gift we can give, to ourselves and to others. After all, if we are all made in the image and likeness of God, as it tells us in Genesis 1:27, coming to a full recognition and appreciation of who we, and others, really are, is an awakening of the highest magnitude. (8) And just maybe, as more and more of us awaken, the anguish felt by those cycling through failure, weakness, illness, abandonment, fear and ignorance could be better buffered and utilized for transformative awakening of society as a whole instead of as a soul-crushing sense of defeat and hopelessness.

When any one of us falls, we all fall. But, when any one of us awakens, we all awaken. We are all connected to one another, whether we recognize it yet or not. If you find yourself on the left-hand side of this equation, know that you are not alone AND that there is *always* the light of dawn after the dark night. If you are fortunate enough to find yourself on the right-hand side of this equation, give thanks for your abundance AND look for others to share it with. As my wife Lisa puts it so eloquently, "True compassion is understanding that Darkness is Darkness and not judging the circumstances that turned out the light." (9)

In spite of all its terror-inducing ways, the Dark Night of the Spirit is also incredibly liberating. Coming to a place where you can identify and follow your own afflatus, yet still be able to step back and allow God/Source/Universe to do Its part, in Its own time, in Its own way, relieves you of an unfathomable degree of responsibility and work. And, by awakening us all to who we really are, it is a gift like no other.

*The best way to make your dreams
come true is to wake up.*
Paul Valéry (10)

May you all someday awaken to who you, and others, really are, to your own Divinity and the Divinity within others. As always, Always Believe In Your Dreams!!!

Weathering Accidental Enlightenment

Chapter 15

The "Zero's Journey"

...and I am reduced to dust and ashes.
Bible (1)

As you may have gathered after reading Chapter 13, Weathering The "Dark Nights" – A Tale of Two Survivors, my wife Lisa and I share a rather unusual level of closeness and compatibility. For over twenty years, we have always done everything together, 24 hours/day, 7 days/week. We worked together; she was the office manager of my chiropractic practice. We parented together, attending every major event in our children's lives. We have even shared a single vehicle together for fifteen out of the past twenty years. And, while some might find the amount of time we spent together excessive, neither of us could imagine life any other way. Lisa completes me in every way and is truly the love of my life.

So, when the Dark Night of the Spirit came to roost and everything I had worked so hard to accomplish, everything of value in my life, was forcibly stripped away from me, our time together was not spared either. After five months of intensive job hunting, following our near foreclosures, and over seventy resume submissions, Lisa finally found work as the office manager for a busy medical practice, working ten to twelve hour days to earn what I used to generate in under an hour's time. Our waking time together was slashed to a mere twelve hours per week during the weekdays, with two and a half hours of that taken up by my shuttling her to and from her new place of employment. I was left alone to handle the unpleasant tasks of shuttering the practice: selling, storing or purging its contents and prepping the building for sale in a mad-dash effort to outrun the mounting storm of sheriff sale that was evermore bearing down on us for delinquent property taxes.

> *Love knows not its own depth*
> *until the hour of separation.*
> **Kahlil Gibran (2)**

People who have suffered the amputation of a limb commonly report experiencing "phantom" limb pains where they experience extreme pain in the area where the limb has been amputated, as if it is still attached to their body. I can only begin to describe the very real physical, emotional and spiritual pain that I felt following this drastic reduction in time spent with Lisa as being akin to phantom limb pain. I could still feel her presence, as though she was still by my side, but she was not there. Any further attempts to put into words the indescribable pain and anguish that this caused to my soul would be impossible to meaningfully convey.

And you would not have to be a rocket-scientist to have surmised from Chapter 13, the experience of the Dark Night of the Spirit is anguishingly painful, in and of itself. But the colossal loss of my time together with Lisa was nearly more than I could bear. Many a time, I prayed to be taken from my torment, to be "returned to sender," so to speak. Often, I found myself teary-eyed, questioning "Why?"

The thought of suicide is a great consolation: by means of it one gets successfully through many a bad night.
Friedrich Nietzsche (3)

In his interpretive tome, <u>Dark Night of the Soul</u>, Saint John of the Cross states, "the soul must needs be in all its parts reduced to a state of emptiness, poverty and abandonment and must be left dry and empty and in darkness... He (God) is purging the soul, annihilating it, emptying it or consuming in it all the *affections* and imperfect habits which it has contracted in its whole life... Here God greatly humbles the soul in order that He may afterwards greatly exalt it." (4) <u>The Works of Mencius</u>, a Confucian philosopher whose classic Chinese work dates from the second half of the 4th century B.C., approximately 1900 years before Saint John of the Cross, considers

Weathering Accidental Enlightenment

"trials and hardships the way in which Heaven prepares men for great services." It states, "when Heaven is about to confer a great office on any man, it first exercises his mind with suffering, and his sinews and bones with toil. It exposes his body to hunger, and subjects him to extreme poverty. It confounds his undertakings. By all these methods it stimulates his mind, hardens his nature, and supplies his incompetencies." (5) Other spiritual masters and authors discuss the need for shedding one's ego before spiritual enlightenment can take place. Khalil Gibran writes in The Prophet, "For even as Love crowns you so shall He crucify you. Even as He is for your growth so is He for your pruning... He threshes you to make you naked. He sifts you to free you from your husks... All of these things shall Love do unto you that you may know the secrets of your heart... Your pain is the breaking of the shell that encloses your understanding." (6)

To recognize your insignificance is enlightenment.
Lao Tzu (7)

Famed mythologist Joseph Campbell talks about the "hero's journey" as a blueprint for the unfoldment of following your bliss. Essentially, each and every one of us are likened to tribal warriors or explorers who depart on some journey, encounter obstacles and adversity, fight the big fight, conquer our demons and then return home to share all that we have learned with the rest of our tribe. Everybody cycles through varying stages and degrees of this journey throughout their lifetime.

My foray into the Dark Night of the Spirit felt much more like the "zero's journey" as I witnessed the complete decimation of my roles and identities as a doctor, business owner, author-speaker-coach, provider for my family and contributor to society. I lost my chosen livelihood and my cherished lifestyle, all of my wealth and my wealth-making capability. It was as though God/Source/Universe had reduced my very existence to absolute zero! How many of you have ever been the last to get picked for a sports team or event, as a kid, and had the two sides fight over who gets stuck with you? Imagine that same scenario as an adult, except that you have now been rejected by Team Life. It seemed to me that Life had pulled me from the game and stuck me in a permanent "time out." If, in fact, part of the purpose of the Dark Night of the Soul is the reduction and destruction of the ego, since it is our ego that fights our ability to ALLOW, then mission accomplished! Perhaps one of the best expressions of the "zero's journey" can be found in the words of Biblical sufferer Job when he stated, "...and I am reduced to dust and ashes," where "dust and ashes" were symbolic of humiliation and insignificance. (8)

To become a nothingness is the door to truth.
Nothingness itself is the means, the goal and attainment.
Osho's 5th Commandment (9)

Lao Tzu states, "When I let go of what I am, I become what I might be." (10) I believe he is talking here about our *attachments*, our *"outward clinging of the spirit"* as Saint John of the Cross called it. (11) Meister Eckhart, a German theologian, philosopher and mystic who lived three hundred years before Saint John of the Cross, believed that the only function of hell was to burn away the part of you that won't let go of your life, your *attachments*. He saw it as a means of freeing your soul. With respect to the Dark Night of the Soul, Dr. Gerald May states, "It's always a process of liberation from *attachment*... and the realization of one's true identity in God." (12) Tibetan Buddhism teaches that our *attachments* are one of the primary causes of all suffering, referring to them as "poisons" or "fires."

Saint John of the Cross viewed the Dark Night of the Soul, along with its associated sense of abandonment, as a gift from God designed specifically to free us from our *attachments*. Contemporary spiritual teacher Eckhart Tolle, on the other hand, describes a more self-imposed isolation caused by our inner resistance to what is; with the only way out to be found by surrendering to what is and releasing our *attachments*. Whether you adhere to Saint John of the Cross' belief in a loving presence that has chosen you, or Eckhart Tolle's more secular view, the "gift" contained within the Dark Night of the Soul is the same.

Each and every one of us are children of God/Source/Universe. As it states in Genesis 1:27, "God made man in His own image." (13) Thus, we are all reflections of Divinity, nothing more AND nothing less! Because there is nowhere where God is not, this means that each and every one of us are reflections of EVERYTHING! Perhaps the real "original sin" is to be found merely in our denial of our never-ending connection to, our communion with, Divinity. Forgetting who we really are, we succumb to a lack consciousness in every arena of our lives, desperately grasping for "our share" before somebody else claims it as "their own." Our *attachments* to things, people, identities, accomplishments, outcomes and ideas limit and imprison our souls. When we let go of our rigidly held limited ideas about who we think we are, we ALLOW ourselves to be the physical manifestation of God-in-man that we were created to be.

Weathering Accidental Enlightenment

Sages and masters throughout the ages have said that you have to let it all go before you can have it all. Ram Dass calls it "The most exquisite paradox… as soon as you give it all up, you can have it all. As long as you want power, you can't have it. The minute you don't want power, you'll have more than you ever dreamed possible." (14) Neale Donald Walsch, author of <u>Conversations with God</u>, agrees, stating, "until you can let go of everything, you will find it hard to hold onto anything. Detachment is the key." (15) However, when you are in the thick of a Dark Night, it feels more like you are just letting everything go. Period. No rebound, no rebirth, just finality as you plummet to the depths of absolute zero.

> *Detachment is not that you should own nothing, but that nothing should own you.*
> **Ali ibn-Abi-Talib (16)**

Traveling along this "zero's journey" is very much akin to dying while you are still alive. You are forced to witness the dismantling of everything you worked so hard your whole life for. It is very reminiscent of the dismantling of an estate of a deceased person. Everything you built rapidly disintegrates before your very eyes. It can seem as though you are being forced to witness, and even participate in, erasing the memories of your very existence: purging, selling off or having taken away all that you worked so hard to acquire or accomplish.

The only real peace comes from completely letting go. You can either let go of your attachments voluntarily, which is sad in and of itself or you can continue to have them ripped violently away from you, which is anguishingly more painful. Either way, you have to let it all go. As those who work in hospice quickly learn, death is peaceful.

Letting go of all of your attachments also brings great clarity to your life. Devoid of all of your attachments, you can finally see your true self. Asking yourself questions such as the following can help speed you along on this stretch of the journey:
- "Who would I be without my money?"
- "Who would I be without my stuff?"
- "Who would I be without my titles?"
- "Who would I be without my accomplishments?"
- "Who would I be without my labels?"

The Dark Night of the Soul is all about pain, suffering and loss. Yet, out of all that, from the ashes that used to be your life, hopefully, like the Greek mythological phoenix, you emerge as more

Weathering Accidental Enlightenment

than you were when you started. Through the process of being reduced to absolute zero, you are freed to be the perfect reflection of the infinite field of loving possibilities that is God/Source/Universe. You can live into the never ending stream of unconditional love that is your true identity, the Source from whence you came.

Not knowing when the dawn will
come, I open every door.
Emily Dickinson (17)

There are numerous other descriptions and titles that the Coming of the Dawn is known by including: stepping into the light, reaching enlightenment, restitution, the Miracle, the Resurrection, the Great Exaltation, and the extension of Grace. The literary term for it is *Deus ex machina*, from Latin, meaning "God from the machine;" whereby Divine intervention literally snatches victory from the jaws of defeat, bringing the story to a happy ending. However, for approximately six million Jewish people during the time of the Holocaust, thousands of Native Americans during the settling of America and thousands upon thousands more Africans during the time of slavery, following their "reduction to dust and ashes," the only Dawn that likely ever came was death. People like Viktor Frankl, Nelson Mandela, Mother Teresa and His Holiness the 14th Dalai Lama, all Dark Night survivors, are very much the exception, not the rule, barely approximating the 1-2% made reference to in Chapter 3, Finding Your AFFLATUS.

> *He that cannot endure the bad*
> *will not live to see the good.*
> **Yiddish Proverb (18)**

I look around me and I am truly humbled by the never-ending stream of blessings before me. Twelve years ago, I was hooked up to a ventilator, hovering between life and death, following a ruptured appendix that had turned to peritonitis and gone septic. EVERY breath I get to take is such sweet nectar! I am profoundly thankful for EVERYTHING in my life today including the bill collectors, auditors, naysayers and critics (ALL of whom I still call "friends and family"). Getting to interact with all of them means that I'm still standing!!! Support and love has come from many unexpected, much appreciated directions. Even the forced time apart from the love of my life, my "ideal" soul mate, Lisa, has come with a silver lining. After more than twenty-two years together, our love for one another, our bond, has ultimately been forged stronger than ever!

Reverend Henry Ward Beecher states, "No man will ever walk through this life and reverse the experience, 'Man that is born of woman is of few days, and full of trouble.' It comes to us all:

Weathering Accidental Enlightenment

not to make us sad, but to make us sober; not to make us sorry, but to make us wise; not to make us despondent, but by its darkness to refresh us, as the night refreshes the day; not to impoverish us, but to enrich us, as the plough enriches the field — to multiply our joy, as the seed is multiplied an hundredfold by planting." (19)

During the writing of <u>The "Zero's Journey"</u>, it became readily apparent that one of two scenarios was taking place: either I was being "groomed" for something far bigger than even I could comprehend or I was being not so slowly incinerated by Life itself! Should this book make it successfully into published form, you will know that a higher purpose was served through all of this and, by providing a roadmap for fellow travelers, my struggles were, in fact, worthwhile to us all. And, if it never sees the light of print, then none will have been erroneously misled.

I AM IGNORANT of absolute truth.
But, I am humble before my ignorance
and therein lies my honor and my reward.
Kahlil Gibran (20)

Afterward

Crossing the "Fault Line"

Once you are capable of knowing, life holds you accountable as if you do know, even when you don't.
George Addair (1)

Just like you can't hold a child responsible for what they don't know because they have not been taught or shown, you can not be held responsible for what you were never taught or shown. Literally, you may have been a "victim" of your own ignorance up until this point in your life. Now, once you have read this book, you do know! From here forward, you no longer need to suffer as a victim of your own ignorance. As I aptly titled the first chapter in <u>iContractor 1</u> concerning your results in life, "It's All Your Fault!" (2) This is great news. Once you cross the "fault line" you can take back your responsibility AND your "response-*ability*;" you can reclaim your power.

    Remember, this is NOT about finding and placing blame. As <u>The Book of Job</u> reminds us, bad things *CAN AND DO* happen to good people! (3) Rather, this is about identifying the areas in your life where you *can* exert some influence. There is an old wisdom that says to focus on what you can control, not on those things that you

Weathering Accidental Enlightenment

cannot. This whole book has been about identifying those factors you can control and then influencing them intentionally. Regardless of the situations and circumstances that you encounter in life, they can all always contribute to your own personal growth IF you CHOOSE to utilize them for such.

Each and every one of you has Divinity within you. Denying your true nature does not make it any less so. In my personal, humbled opinion, it is still better to risk losing everything pursuing your afflatus than to keep it all by living a lie! Once you come to realize, however, that the ONLY thing you ever really can lose is your sense of self, your decision becomes a simple one.

You will need broad shoulders to cross the fault line but you can do it. I have complete and total faith in you. Everything rests on your shoulders from here forward! Welcome fellow earth-bound travelers of light!

Epilogue

20¢ worth of Philosophy
1 Year Later

One never goes so far as when one doesn't know where one is going.
Johann Wolfgang von Goethe (1)

As discussed at the beginning of this book, our paradigms, not "pair of dimes," define and constrict our world-view. Everything we experience is filtered through our individual paradigms and everything we do becomes tainted by them. Some paradigms are so vast as to encompass most others. Such is the case with ADIO versus OIBU.

ADIO ("Above-Down, Inside-Out") says that everything originates from a "Higher Power," above and beyond us, and is then channeled down through us, from inside-out; from God to and through man- and woman-kind.

OIBU ("Outside-In, Below-Up"), on the other hand, says that everything originates outside of, separate and apart from, us and then travels into us and upwards toward God.

Weathering Accidental Enlightenment

ADIO is more aligned with Eastern thought. It is based upon seeing life as whole and vitalistic in nature, as a living entity with meaning and purpose; mind and body are inseparably one. By its very nature, a vitalistic Universe is one filled with wonder and possibility; where anything can happen; where sometimes we *can* influence outcomes.

OIBU is more aligned with Western thought. It is based upon the mechanistic viewpoint, espoused by French philosopher René Descartes three centuries ago, that separated the non-physical and the physical, the non-measurable and the measurable, the mind and the body into distinct entities. The entire Universe is constrained by rigid laws and limited possibilities relegating us to nothing more than cogs in an accidentally formed clock.

Most of us, in the Western world at least, have been so indoctrinated into the OIBU paradigm that we are unable to see life in any other way. Our lives have become permeated on every level by a profound sense of lack and hopelessness. We routinely turn to drugs & surgeries seeking "health," ministers & meditative prayer seeking "salvation" and self-help gurus & experts seeking "secrets" to success. We have grown accustomed to looking for superheroes to rescue us from our woes. We have lost our faith; faith that the same power that created us also heals us, saves us and guides us to our afflatus. In spite of the message consistently found within the spiritual texts referenced throughout <u>The "Zero's Journey,"</u> works spanning thousands of years, we are forever looking outside of ourselves for answers. However, the most that we can benefit from any of these aforementioned outside-in sources is to supplant our fear with hope. And that is a gift we are capable of giving to ourselves in the first place. As Dorothy found out seventy-five years ago in Oz, she had what she was seeking, buried deep inside of her, all along. She only had to wake up to its ever-present existence and so do you.

The world goes up and the world goes down,
the sunshine follows the rain;
and yesterday's sneer and yesterday's frown
can never come over again.
Charles Kingsley (2)

Everything about the manner in which I have endeavored to live my life for over twenty years now has been predicated upon the ADIO philosophy. It is why I chose to study Chiropractic in the first place. It is what compels me to still write. There is an old wisdom that suggests that times may be tough if your neighbor loses their job, but times are not catastrophic until you lose

Weathering Accidental Enlightenment

yours. While my wife Lisa managed to find work outside of our chiropractic office after four months of intensive searching, it took me a full sixteen months to find a paying job of my own. Over eighty resumes were sent out, covering a wide variety of vocations; more than fifty publishers and agents were contacted and numerous speaking opportunities were aggressively pursued, all the while still trying to resuscitate my feebled chiropractic practice. From all of that, only two companies expressed any interest whatsoever in replying to me. Ultimately, I found work in accounting, now working seventy to eighty hours to earn what I used to generate in only seven to eight hours, and narrowly escaping our impending tax sale just a few short months before the scheduled sale date. When all was said and done, it was as though the past twenty-two years' worth of schooling, effort, hopes and dreams had all been erased; with seemingly nothing more to show for it than a tired, old body and nearly half a million dollars in debt.

At this point, some of you may be wondering, "If only 1-2% succeed, what's the point?" Henry David Thoreau says, "What you get by achieving your goals is not as important as what you become by achieving your goals." (3) I would take that one step further and add that, regardless of whether or not you achieve your goals, who you become by striving to achieve them is what matters the most. That is what ultimately up-levels humanity.

Jake Ducey, author of Into The Wind, states, "Life has no intention of punishing anyone for making the choice to follow their heart." (4) However, neither does Life (God/Source/Universe) necessarily guarantee your successful accomplishment. The only gifts "guaranteed" to you are as follows:
- a.) Having a dream, an afflatus, to follow in the first place.
- b.) The freedom to exercise your choice of attitude in any and every given circumstance which, as mentioned previously, allows you, no matter what circumstances or outcomes present themselves, to always make them "for" you.

The best laid schemes o' Mice an' Men
Gang aft agley
[Often stated as: The best laid plans of Mice and Men / Often go awry]
Robert Burns (5)

Aristotle believed in a process he coined as "entelechy" whereby a vital force directed an organism toward self-fulfillment; in essence, *towards* realized afflatus. Life wants, in fact, demands, that you follow your afflatus so you can become who you were meant to be. Whether or not you actually succeed in realizing your afflatus is beside the point. Life's only intention is for your spiritual development and growth. This can happen "with" your voluntary participation OR it can happen "to" you as you go kicking and screaming through your own "zero's journey" toward inevitable enlightenment.

> *It's only by forgetting yourself that you draw near to God.*
> **Henry David Thoreau (6)**

The Bible tells us that Jesus ministered primarily to those who could not help themselves, whether through fault of their own or not, due to illness, poverty, bad life choices or whatever. Through the levels of humility and compassion that the "zero's journey" awakens in us, we are placed in a position to do as Jesus did for the suffering who are all around us; not in blasphemy but rather, enabling and ennobling us to actually be the hands of God at work in our world. I can think of no higher calling to any of us than this.

> *Help your brother's boat across, and*
> *your own will reach the shore.*
> **Hindu Proverb (7)**

So where do we go from here? We do as we have *always* done. We get up, we show up and we give 100% of our best effort, no matter what. And thus, like the mythological phoenix, we have the opportunity to rise yet again!

Weathering Accidental Enlightenment

About the Author

Dr. Ketcham was in private practice as a chiropractor for over seventeen and a half years. He was asked to contribute a quarterly philosophy column to his hometown newspaper, The Meadville Tribune (circ. 12,000), in the Active for Life supplement, from 2009 until 2013. Prior to that, as part of a 10-year long collaborative effort by all of the local chiropractors, he contributed articles once or twice a year to The Meadville Tribune's monthly HealthBeat column. Additionally, he is the author of iContractor 1, a book he self-published in 2012.

Ralph Waldo Emerson said: "Make your own Bible. Select and collect all the words and sentences that in all your reading have been to you like the blast of triumph out of Shakespeare, Seneca, Moses, John and Paul." (1)

The iContractor book series is Dr. Ketcham's "Bible."

Dr. Ketcham is also a motivational speaker who delivers a powerful message of taking personal responsibility for your results in life and changing those results by changing yourself from the inside-out!

Weathering Accidental Enlightenment

"In order for things to change and improve, you don't need a 'change of venue.' What you need is a 'change within you'." (iContractor 1, p. 42)

However, when it comes right down to it, Dr. Ketcham is the first to acknowledge, "I am nobody; no better, no worse than anybody else. I am just doing the best I can with the resources I find before me, just like everybody else." In fact, rather than puffing out his chest and touting his credentials, he prefers the simple title of "jon," as he aspires to serve as a dream re-kindler to his fellow earth-bound travelers of light.

Much like Job from the Bible, jon has known more than his fair share of adversity and misfortune. Having gone broke 3X within 4 years, nearly dying from a life-threatening illness and skirting perilously close to homelessness, he immersed himself into a decade-long study of personal development and success that included reading over 100 classic works, repeatedly listening to more than two dozen audio programs and watching over a dozen videos. He was then able to turn his life around and build the "waiting-list" chiropractic practice of his dreams, only to have his entire livelihood mostly evaporate following sweeping insurance company reductions in Pennsylvania in 2012 that took most of the fun and ALL of the viability out of private practice. By documenting his journey into hell and back, he leaves a trail of light to illuminate the way out for others still lost in the abyss of darkness.

jon lives in "wooded bliss" surrounded by 35 acres of dense forestland in Meadville, Pennsylvania. Additionally, he is the President of the once thriving chiropractic practice, Ketcham Chiropractic, PLLC. He has two beautiful, gifted children: a twenty-year-old son, who is a talented science fiction author/artist and a seventeen-year-old daughter, who is a gifted musician. He shares his home with one basset hound, one chihuahua, ten cats, one guinea pig, a cockatiel, a bunny and five chickens! Nearly all of his pets are "rescues."

jon's articles have been well received and are also available by following his blogs at:

www.TheZerosJourney.com
and
www.AlwaysBelieveInYourDreams.com.

Deluxe, Hardcover Edition of this text, with hand-sewn integral satin bookmark, is also available exclusively via these two web addresses.

Weathering Accidental Enlightenment

Connecting to Dr. Ketcham

Websites:
TheZerosJourney.com
- Follow The "Zero's Journey" Blog
- Subscribe to The "Zero's Journey" Newsletter

AlwaysBelieveInYourDreams.com
- "Book the Doc" to speak at your next event!
- Subscribe to "Doc's Newsletter"
- Follow "Doc's Blog"
- Get coached by the Doc

Facebook Pages:
Facebook.com/thezerosjourney
Facebook.com/drketcham

LinkedIn:
Dr. Jon M. Ketcham

Weathering Accidental Enlightenment

Appendix A

Constructive Concepts: Words to Live By from The "Zero's Journey"

Preface

- I write and speak because I have a message burning inside of me, a message so powerful that it will consume me from within if I don't acquiesce and let it out to be shared with others, others just like you!
- You are held back, like a prisoner in shackles, by anything you do not understand.
- you already possess everything you are currently in search of, everything you think you need to live the life of your dreams. All of the power and magic that exist in the Universe are already perfectly reflected in your very being at this very moment.
- Once you get your inner house in order, constructing your dream life will take care of itself.

Chapter 1

Weathering Accidental Enlightenment

- In my humble opinion, the classic works of Ralph Waldo Trine [In Tune With The Infinite], Wallace Wattles [The Science of Getting Rich], Charles Haanel [The Master Key System], Napoleon Hill [Think And Grow Rich], Rhonda Byrne [The Secret] and even myself [iContractor 1] are **all** slightly off-base, missing the final obvious, yet subtle, conclusion that there is no such thing as the Law of Attraction! None whatsoever!
- the Law of "Attraction" is really a misnomer since like does not attract like.
- In spite of its seemingly miraculous ability to help some people to improve their station in life, the Law of Attraction is based upon principles that defy the known laws of physics, chemistry and physiology AND that deny the word of God (and numerous other spiritual teachers and teachings, including sacred Hindu texts and Tibetan Buddhist precepts); based on these two flawed assumptions: like attracts like and you are lacking in some way.
- The Law of Attraction can not possibly be an accurate depiction of reality!
- There may be no such thing as the Law of Attraction BUT perhaps there is a Law of *Reflection*.

- Like may not attract like but like DOES reflect like!
- Consider this, if we are all spiritual beings of light and whatever we emit is what gets reflected back to us via the Law of Reflection, doesn't it make sense to focus more on who you are being on the inside, what you are emitting, than what you think is missing on the outside that you think you must attract?
- who you are being on the inside shines outward and gets reflected back to you from the mirror of God, on a massive, magnified scale, as the people, events and circumstances of your life through the Law of Reflection.
- If you find yourself in want it is likely because you have forgotten who you are.
- It is impossible to be lacking in any way unless we ourselves make it so. We have enough already. We are enough already!
- This is why practicing "gratitude in advance" is so powerful. It enables us to embrace the fact that, whatever it is that we want, we **already** have it. And THAT is what gets reflected back to us!
- Who we surround ourselves with affects who we reflect and who reflects us. The more negative influences we are reflecting

back to others, the less our own light can shine through.
- You maximize your light by being true to you.
- Know this, you already have everything you need inside of you. The sooner you recognize this, the sooner you will emit it via your thoughts, feelings/emotions and actions. And then, that is what will get reflected back to you as the people, events and circumstances of your life through the Law of Reflection.

Chapter 2

- I would posit that 98% of them are doomed to fail for lack of an understanding that lasting, positive change and growth requires an essential, sequential, 3-step process.
- Most people develop very constipated, restrictive views of themselves based upon labels they use to define and confine their capabilities.
- In light of this, two things should become readily apparent: first, we are not limited in our capabilities in any way other than those limits we create for ourselves and second, any longings, desires, passions, interests and talents we have are, as reflections of God, meant to be celebrated and utilized, not stifled and constricted.

- In fact, denying our innermost longings is denying God Himself!
- Understand this, trying to improve yourself without first knowing yourself is like wanting to plan a trip to a foreign country but without regard for where you will be starting from.
- Only by first knowing where you are at can you then create a workable strategy to get where you want to go.
- If you don't love who you are already, changing the "package" that your container is will not change that.
- Not loving yourself, as you already are, is criticizing the work of God!
- God doesn't need you to believe in Him. God "*is*" with or without your belief. God wants you to believe in yourselves!
- The bottom line is this, you will NEVER let yourself accomplish something that you don't feel you deserve, not for very long at least.
- Now, spend the time and effort necessary to fully appreciate the individuation of God in man that is you!
- "HOW" you do what you do is infinitely more important than "WHAT" you actually do.

Weathering Accidental Enlightenment

- Is "HOW" you are currently being, on the inside, consistent with "WHAT" you are hoping to accomplish?
- Because life can only mirror back to you what you have previously put out there, the only way to create a better life is by creating a better image, a better "I am"-age to have life reflect back to you.
- In other words, be **now** HOW you want to be when you are successful and you will be successful **now**!
- live every day as a "come as you will be" party.
- Engage in activities now that create the feeling of having your dreams already accomplished. Find ways to awaken to the fact that you have already arrived. You are already there!

Chapter 3

- Your innermost dreams and longings are not the result of random chance or circumstance. They exist within your soul because they have been Divinely communicated to you from God; they are YOUR afflatus, impelling you from within.
- Finding and following your afflatus requires that you quiet the voices of doubt in your mind and, instead, listen to the wee small voice within your soul. It requires that you

learn to ignore the naysayers and societal pressures for conformity and, instead, each travel your own path ALONE.
- My turnaround, if you will, began when I made the decision to live.
- If you are having trouble finding your afflatus, start by living your life passionately. When you live your life with passion, often your passion, your afflatus, finds you!
- Your afflatus is already inside of you too! All you have to do is uncover and honor it; strip away the extraneous patterns, personas and limits that have accumulated from society, upbringing and self-doubt.
- Your music, your afflatus, has not gone away. It's still inside each and every one of you.
- If you listen to the melody of your soul, it will not lead you astray.
- Now is just as good a time as any to find and follow your afflatus. In fact, NOW is the only time you've got!

Chapter 4

- every one of you, if you live long enough, will eventually experience hardship and loss on some level. When this happens, you will be faced with two choices: you can either let it **define and destroy** you OR you can use

Weathering Accidental Enlightenment

it to **strengthen and empower** you; you can either let yourself become hardened and closed by bitterness or you can become softened and opened *with loving compassion*. You get to choose via your response.

- Those of you who allow each and every obstacle and hardship to define and destroy you will suffer the effects from a self-imposed imprisonment by the thoughts and feelings/emotions that you have chosen: blame-by-blame, justification-by-justification, excuse-by-excuse, complaint-by-complaint. But know this, you are your own jailer!
- When you let hardship of any kind define you, it's all you think about, it's all you talk about, it's what you become about and eventually, it is going to take you out!
- The ONE thing, which is the ONLY thing, you have any real control over is your ATTITUDE OF MIND... and that is the ONLY thing you need to change in order to change EVERYTHING!
- I would say that life happens "for" them If AND ONLY IF, no matter what happens, they **choose** to look for the benefit and thereby make it "for" them.
- Fear is nothing more than faith in a negative outcome; backwards faith, if you will.

- F.E.A.R., to me, says to "Forget Everything And Run!"
- By focusing always and only on the positive, no matter what happens to or around you, it *will* always be "for" you, containing positive elements.
- Faith and belief are ALL about carrying yourself and behaving in a manner where there is not a shred of evidence to support your views. So is insanity. Enjoy the ride!
- Go out into the world expecting to be fully supported in your dreams and give thanks both for the ride and for already having arrived!

Chapter 5

- Trying to "force" outcomes is definitely not an act of faith.
- Getting "lost at SEE," as my wife calls it; in other words, "I'll believe it when I see it!" is not an act of faith either.
- Faith is an unrelenting journey through the "Dark Night of the Soul" that refuses to concede defeat, refuses to succumb to the "night terrors" and refuses to give up.
- Faith is not having a "back-up" plan, not having a "plan B."
- Faith is 100% commitment; it's not partial and it's not casual.

Weathering Accidental Enlightenment

- A curious phenomenon often times occurs when you commit yourself 100% to your afflatus: before your afflatus shows any signs of life whatsoever, EVERYTHING else seems to go South!
- Only the strength of my faith, fueled by the burning passion and clarity of my vision were likely to see me through.
- One of life's harshest lessons is coming to terms with the fact that you must perpetually fight for all that you hold dear if you want to make it through successfully. It does not matter who you are or what you have accomplished previously, you must NEVER give up fighting for everything you desire to be, do and have; for everything you desire to achieve. In fact, in the very moment you want to give up, that is when you must give it all you've got. That is when you are on the brink of your biggest breakthroughs.
- Faith requires that you persist through the darkness where you cannot see, with nothing more to illumine your path or soothe your troubled soul than the belief that, as long as you continue to show up, always being and doing your very best, better days lie ahead for you. If you can accomplish this one task, you will have succeeded where most others have failed!

Chapter 6

- Money is analogous to air and the flow of money is a lot like breathing.
- And to do that, you need to become a new you on the inside because for success, you don't need to go SOMEWHERE else, you just need to *become* SOMEONE else.
- And, a word of caution, if you are chasing virtually any career because it looks "glamorous" to you, you are likely to be looking at it through the blinders of infatuation; what I refer to as "infatuation blinders" or "lala goggles."
- Wealth, in and of itself, is a consciousness. It is a recognition AND acceptance, an allowing, of all of the abundance that already is.
- Part of becoming prosperous and wealthy centers on coming to a recognition that you both *have* "enough" and *are* "enough" already and then being grateful for all you have.
- while I have been financially broke or bankrupt many times, I have NEVER lacked for abundance, prosperity and wealth regardless of whether I recognized and acknowledged such at the time.

Weathering Accidental Enlightenment

- Give without restraint and just breathe, knowing full-well that all you need will be there for you when you need it!

Chapter 7

- life is far too weighty of a matter to be handled without a sense of levity.
- laughter's biggest selling point rests in its ability to moderate unpleasant situations and accompany you as you journey through "the Dark Night of the Soul" on the path to following your afflatus.
- Maintaining your sense of humor, particularly as you journey through "the Dark Night of the Soul," enables you to reclaim a modicum of control over your emotions, control over your response to the circumstances of your life. And, as you choose your responses, you better situate yourself to enjoy the process as you follow the path to your own afflatus.
- laughter is much, much, much more powerful than screams to fuel your life!

Chapter 8

- The very act of trying to "force" an outcome says that you do NOT have faith in God/Source/Universe to answer your prayers and fulfill your desires.

- This "hyper-intention," this tendency to try to "force" outcomes, is typically the end result of your resistance to what "is" combined with your struggles to see a light at the end of the tunnel; a glimmer of luminescence in "the Dark Night of the Soul."
- when you make the decision to believe in a friendly Universe, to believe that God knows what He is doing, that He really is on your side and always has been, then you can stop resisting what is happening. At that point, you are able to stop struggling and raging against all that has already taken place and cannot be altered in any way anyways.
- "Allowing" involves a gentle steering, nudging with desire, whereas "giving up" involves moving from a white-knuckle level of forced control to nothing.
- "Allowing" is based in TRUST and FAITH whereas "giving up" is based in hopelessness, apathy and despondence.
- More than anything else, "allowing" is about letting go of your attachments
- "Allowing" is about expressing your desires WITHOUT making rigid attachments to their fulfillment.
- Most people spend excessive amounts of time and energy fighting what "is" and

trying to "force" outcomes whose time has not yet arrived. When you give up this one-sided fight and endless struggle with yourself, you free up countless resources that you can more productively use in the present moment.

Chapter 9

- Finding and following your afflatus mandates that you step out of line and learn to think for yourself from here forward.
- Resisting what "is" and lamenting what "isn't" causes you to completely miss out on the magic of the moment.
- giving thanks in advance is a VERY powerful exercise, not as a means to "trick" God/Source/Universe into giving you your "stuff" but as a means of recognizing and acknowledging all that *already* is! This is about coming to an inner knowing and acceptance, a FAITH and ALLOWING, of the abundance that is *already* yours. Your "stuff" will show up when you truly and fully recognize and acknowledge that you were never without it in the first place!

Chapter 10

- Far better, in my opinion, to love yourself for who you already are than to perpetually loathe yourself for who you are not.

- You can still change and "improve" yourself if you so desire. But the real starting point has to be from a place of total acceptance, already loving yourself for who you were uniquely created to be.
- Most people fail, not because of their non-conformist tendencies, but rather due to their efforts to conform. By attempting to "fit in," they suppress their true nature. If you know yourself and truly love yourself, how could you possibly deny that?!?

Chapter 11

- As we live into our afflatus, most of us realize that our gifts were never intended solely for us, to be hoarded and kept hidden.
- Life isn't just about YOU, it never was; it's about us, ALL OF US TOGETHER!
- If you want to pay homage to the reflection of Divinity that is within you, then it is imperative that you find your afflatus, follow your afflatus and then live into who God created you uniquely to be.
- Tap into your Divinity and then share it with others.
- Find your own light and then use it to illuminate the path for others who are still struggling to find their way out of the darkness!

- we can override our "reflective" tendency by *intentionally choosing* to recognize the Divinity within others, even those who are not yet aware of it within themselves, and reflect that back to them instead!
- by *intentionally choosing* to recognize the Divinity in others, we are saving lives every day!!!

Chapter 12

- Prayer, as I have come to understand it, can be defined as ANY interior exercise or journey that serves to connect you with your own Divinity.
- "cosmic coincidences" and "serendipitous synchronicities" will become your lifelines, connecting you to something greater than yourself; tethering your sanity in the dark.
- the overriding purpose and value of spirituality lies in encouraging and supporting your cooperation with the plans that God/Source/Universe already has for you and, in actuality, has already begun to initiate in your lives.
- However, not all doors open the same way. There are times in life when you can PUSH through these unlocked doors of opportunity with ease: making plans, setting goals and making measurable progress. And then,

there are times when PUSHING, slamming yourself against these doors that must be PULLED, only causes you to suffer bruising. Learning to recognize which doors to push and which doors to pull might quite possibly be the hardest lesson any of you will ever face.

Chapter 13

- As I understand and have experienced it, Stage I, the Dark Night of the Soul, results directly from what you are emitting. The consequences of your negative thinking and feeling are now being reflected back to you full force.
- Everybody experiences the Dark Night of the Sense during the course of their lifetime, some more frequently and more intensely than others.
- Stage II, the Dark Night of the Spirit, is the far less common and far more intense of the two stages.
- This true crisis of faith is now brought on by the prolonged delay between all of your positive emissions of thought, feeling and action and their subsequent positive reflection back to you.
- It is during this same period that a new level of consciousness is being birthed. Special

Weathering Accidental Enlightenment

care and attention must be given to resist the urge to abort your dreams or let them become stillborn at this time.
- the anguish, pain and mental torment felt during the perceived long lag time between emitted desire/dream/afflatus and its reflected reality is both real and consequential. Hopelessness abounds and suffocates.
- I love having and using all of my stuff *but* I am not my stuff. I AM with and without every last bit of it. Who I have become, or grown into, can NEVER be taken away from me *unless* I choose to surrender it myself!
- I had seen my own mother perish under similar circumstances when I was sixteen years of age… And so, with everything else crumbling around me, it became necessary to also devise a plan to rescue my wife from the bowels of hell.
- Fortunately for the both of us, the simple 3-step process I had created previously, the Always Believe In Your Dreams Coaching (SM) methodology, fit the bill perfectly
- Trust the process of life to unfold without unraveling.
- Allow the sands of time to run without you tonight!

- Not everybody gets to experience the Dark Night of the Spirit. Painful though it is, the birthing of a new level of consciousness is truly a gift.
- As you tap into your own Divinity, the brighter and less impeded your own light becomes, the greater the shadow it can cast!
- Your life will be defined, ultimately, by the choices you make in responding to your own Dark Nights, by who you choose to be, moment-by-precious-moment. Choose in favor of YOU!!!

Chapter 14

- The more I learn about everything, the less, I now realize, I know about anything!
- I am just an ordinary guy, like every one of you, a fellow traveler of light who has read a lot and experienced a whole lot more. But, by no means do I have all of the answers.
- The nature of life is change. And, the more we strive to keep things the same, the greater the changes seem to be.
- the only guarantee in life is that NOTHING is guaranteed!
- if we are all made in the image and likeness of God, as it tells us in Genesis 1:27, coming to a full recognition and appreciation of who we, and others, really

- are, is an awakening of the highest magnitude.
- When any one of us falls, we all fall. But, when any one of us awakens, we all awaken. We are all connected to one another, whether we recognize it yet or not.
- As my wife Lisa puts it so eloquently, "True compassion is understanding that Darkness is Darkness and not judging the circumstances that turned out the light."
- Coming to a place where you can identify and follow your own afflatus, yet still be able to step back and allow God/Source/Universe to do Its part, in Its own time, in Its own way, relieves you of an unfathomable degree of responsibility and work.

Chapter 15

- My foray into the Dark Night of the Spirit felt much more like the "zero's journey" as I witnessed the complete decimation of my roles and identities as a doctor, business owner, author-speaker-coach, provider for my family and contributor to society.
- It seemed to me that Life had pulled me from the game and stuck me in a permanent "time out."
- Perhaps one of the best expressions of the "zero's journey" can be found in the words

The Zero's Journey

of Biblical sufferer Job when he stated, "...and I am reduced to dust and ashes," where "dust and ashes" were symbolic of humiliation and insignificance.
- we are all reflections of Divinity, nothing more AND nothing less!
- Perhaps the real "original sin" is to be found merely in our denial of our never-ending connection to, our communion with, Divinity.
- Our *attachments* to things, people, identities, accomplishments, outcomes and ideas limit and imprison our souls. When we let go of our rigidly held limited ideas about who we think we are, we ALLOW ourselves to be the physical manifestation of God-in-man that we were created to be.
- Traveling along this "zero's journey" is very much akin to dying while you are still alive.
- As those who work in hospice quickly learn, death is peaceful.
- The Dark Night of the Soul is all about pain, suffering and loss. Yet, out of all that, from the ashes that used to be your life, hopefully, like the Greek mythological phoenix, you emerge as more than you were when you started.
- Through the process of being reduced to absolute zero, you are freed to be the perfect

reflection of the infinite field of loving possibilities that is God/Source/Universe.
- for approximately six million Jewish people during the Holocaust, thousands of Native Americans during the settling of America and thousands upon thousands more of Africans during the time of slavery, following their "reduction to dust and ashes," the only Dawn that likely ever came was death.
- EVERY breath I get to take is such sweet nectar! I am profoundly thankful for EVERYTHING in my life today including the bill collectors, auditors, naysayers and critics (ALL of whom I still call "friends and family"). Getting to interact with all of them means that I'm still standing!!!

Afterward
- Regardless of the situations and circumstances that you encounter in life, they can all always contribute to your own personal growth IF you CHOOSE to utilize them for such.

Epilogue
- times may be tough if your neighbor loses their job, but times are not catastrophic until you lose yours.

The Zero's Journey

- regardless of whether or not you achieve your goals, who you become by striving to achieve them is what matters the most. That is what ultimately up-levels humanity.
- Through the levels of humility and compassion that the "zero's journey" awakens in us, we are placed in a position to do as Jesus did for the suffering who are all around us; not in blasphemy but rather, enabling and ennobling us to actually be the hands of God at work in our world.

Weathering Accidental Enlightenment

Appendix B

The "Safety Pin Cycle" – re-visited

[Note: this appendix 1st appeared in <u>iContractor 1</u> and was originally based upon the Law of Attraction. It has been revised here to be in alignment with our new understanding of the Law of Reflection]

In Chiropractic, there is a teaching tool from the 1920s referred to as the "Safety Pin Cycle." (1) Basically, the "Safety Pin Cycle" looks at the function of the nervous system and reduces it down into an easy-to-follow, closed-loop feedback diagram that resembles a safety pin. At the top of the safety pin, you have a brain cell and at the bottom, you have a tissue cell. Nerves connect the brain cell and tissue cell together into a closed-loop feedback system. Motor nerves (efferent transmission) run from the brain cell to the tissue cell, telling the tissue cell what to do. Sensory nerves (afferent transmission) run from the tissue cell up to the brain cell, telling the brain cell about its environment. (See Figure I) For example, let's say that the tissue cell is in your hand. And, let's say that you put your hand onto a hot stove. The sensory nerves transmit information to the brain telling it that your hand is on fire. The brain responds by transmitting along motor nerves to cause muscles to contract pulling your hand from the hot stove.

This same analogy, the Safety Pin Cycle, can be used to explain the Always Believe In Your Dreams Coaching (SM) methodology for applying the Law of Reflection. However, instead of having a brain cell at the top of the safety pin, let's put the "What" that you have decided you want. The bottom of the safety pin will now be your "How", your internal level of being. The motor nerves running from top-to-bottom, "What"-to-"How", reflect "How" you would feel if you already had succeeded in accomplishing your dream. We'll call this your "anticipated post-success feeling." The sensory nerves running from bottom-to-top, "How"-to-"What", we will call your "pre-emptive feeling." This is the "How" feeling, previously identified, that you now must create, in advance of your dream fulfillment. (See Figure II)

To really understand how the Law of Reflection operates, let's now turn the safety pin on its side. The bottom of the safety pin, the "How", now resides squarely in your heart, where all of your feelings originate. And the head of the safety pin, the "What", lies at the interface between your inner world (inner states) and outer world (outer events). This is where the frequency emitted by your thoughts, feelings and actions goes out into the Universe. And, let's place that "What" in the center of a bulls-eye to signify the laser-like focus, precision and clarity you are using by being exquisitely specific in describing exactly what you want. (See Figure III)

Finally, we plug the simple, 3-step Always Believe In Your Dreams Coaching (SM) methodology into our safety pin cycle, replacing the "anticipated post-success feeling" with "Up-level" and replacing "pre-emptive feeling" with "Act 'as if.'" (See Figure IV) Making sure your thoughts, feelings and actions are consistent and in congruence maximizes their reflective intensity.

Now can you see why focusing your efforts on changing your outer world, rather than your inner world, is futile? As Mark Victor Hansen says, life "is an inside→outing rather than an outside→inning." (2) Changing your inner world first (and only) is what changes the quality and quantity of light you are emitting so that what gets reflected back to you, from the mirror of God, is more in alignment with your innermost dreams and aspirations.

Weathering Accidental Enlightenment

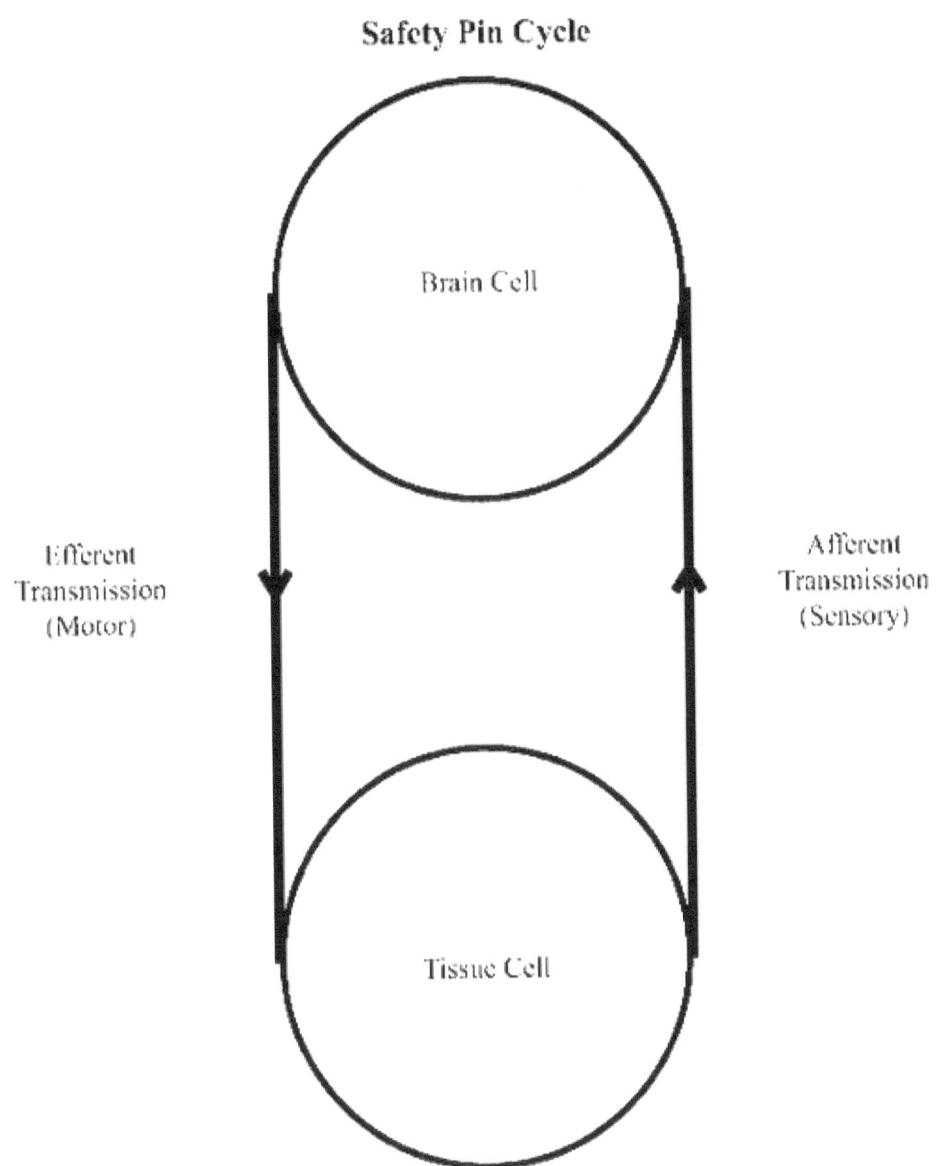

Figure I

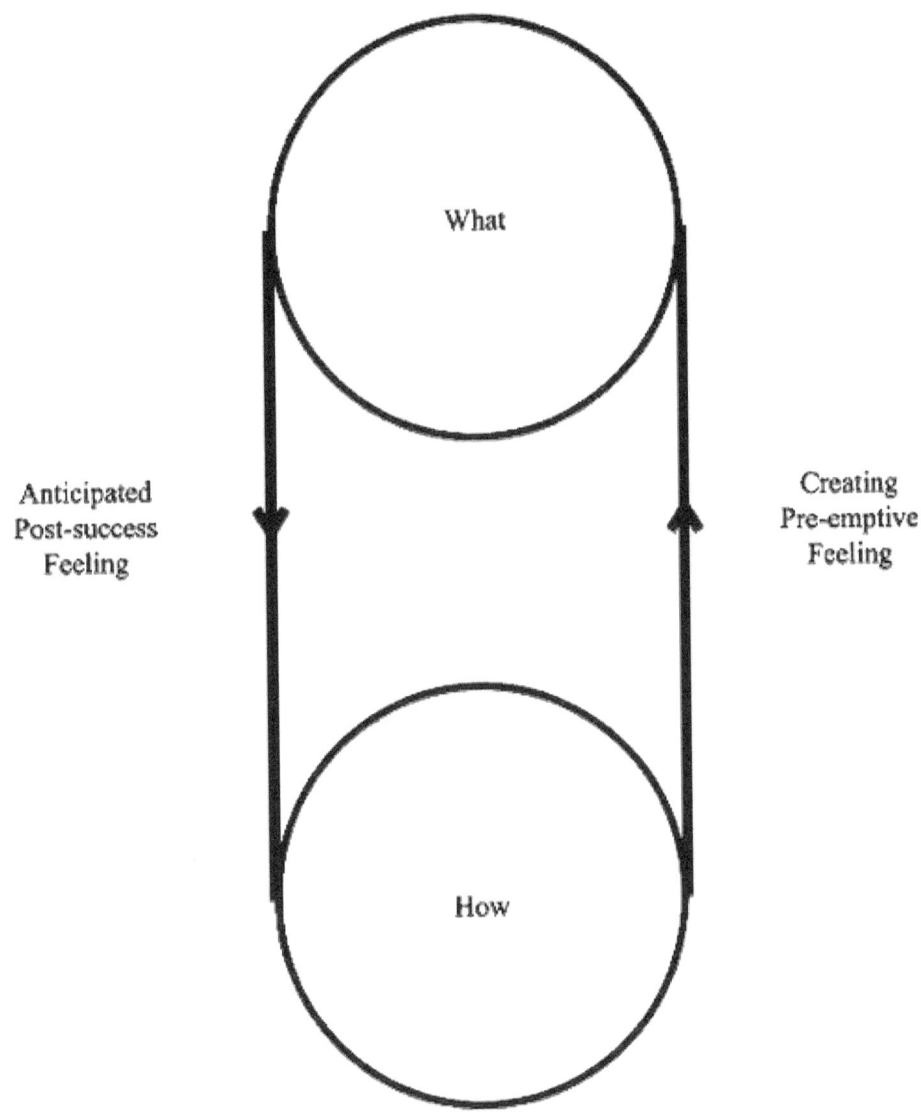

Figure II

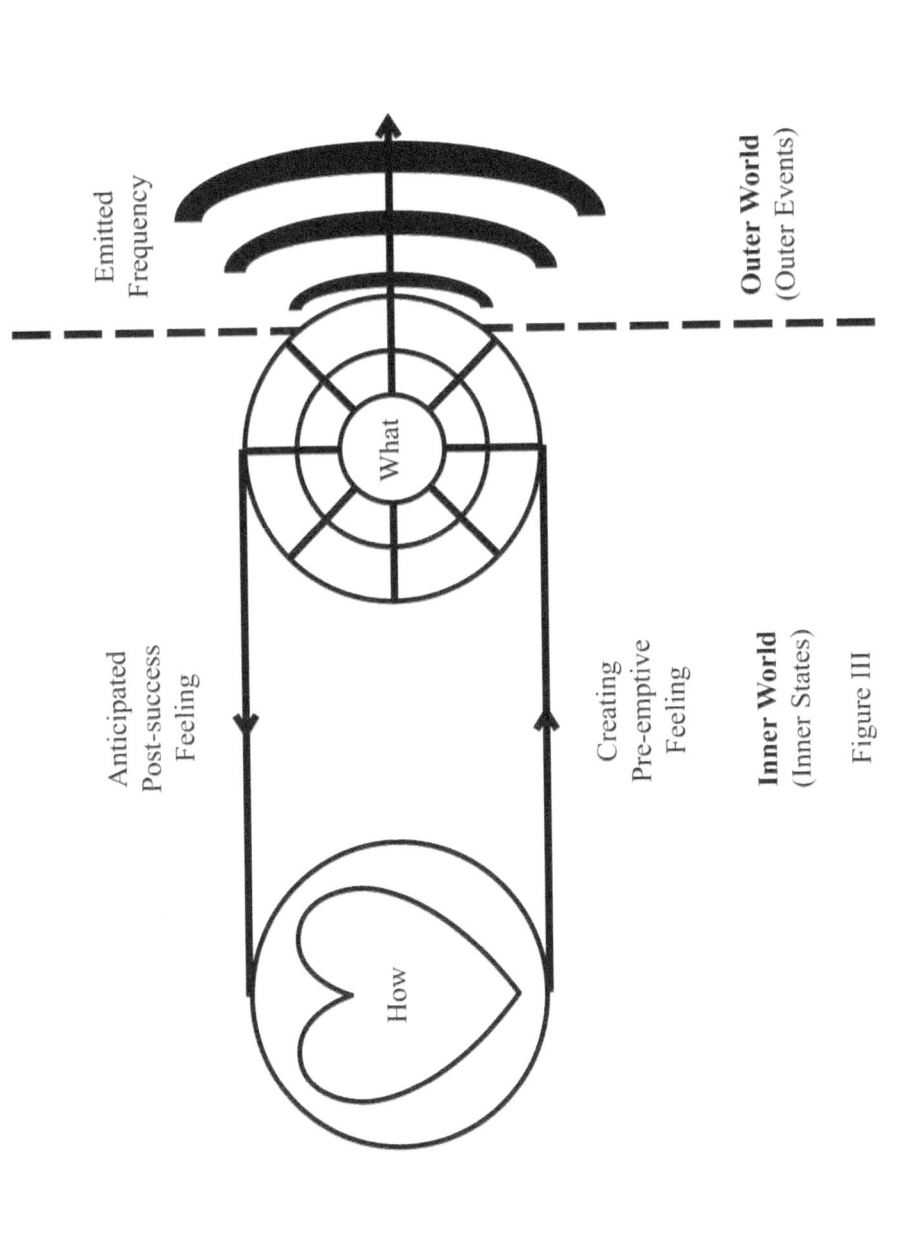

Figure III

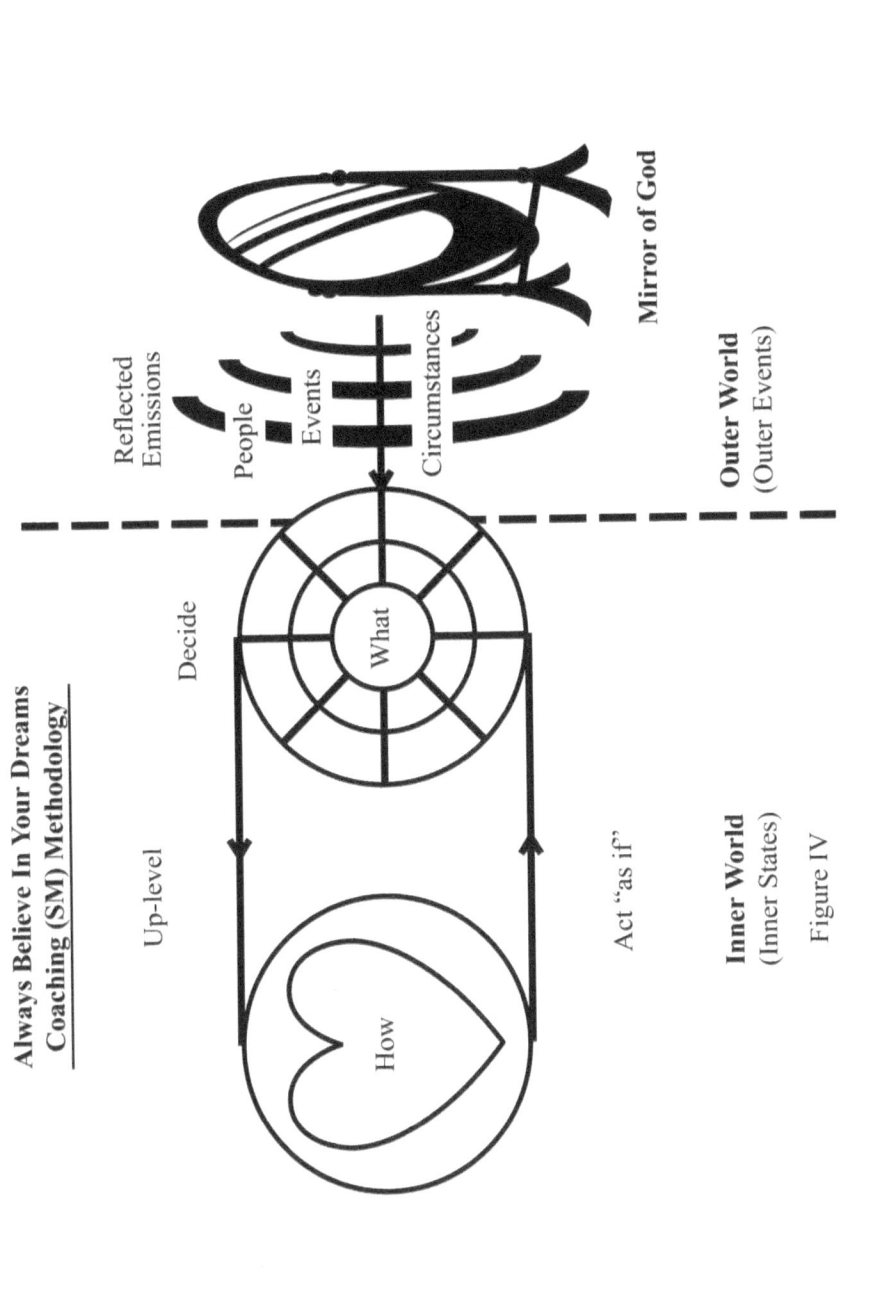

Always Believe In Your Dreams Coaching (SM) Methodology

Figure IV

Appendix C

Being About One's Purpose For Being

The following is a paper I wrote back in 1996 for my 9th Trimester Philosophy class at Palmer College of Chiropractic. Its purpose is to show some of the potential negative physiological consequences of not finding and following your afflatus. Enjoy!

Weathering Accidental Enlightenment

"Being About One's Purpose For Being"

or

Autosuggestional Causation Of The Vertebral Subluxation Complex

Weathering Accidental Enlightenment

"To be or not to be, that is the question." (1) As Shakespeare so aptly described, being about one's purpose for being is a decisional process which ultimately defines the journey we call life.

What?!? One's decisions determine life defined as a miserable existence versus life as an art form? Yes! Everyone is blessed at birth with a certain degree of talents. How one decides to pursue (or not pursue) the development of these talents is the deciding factor.

In order to better understand this, we need to digress for a moment to examine the primitive response referred to as "Fight or Flight." According to Homewood...

- "Into primitive man was built the simple 'fight or flight' mechanism, which demanded expression of fear in a musculo-skeletal activity." (2)
- "By the use of muscles, the stimulus, which caused the unpleasant emotion of fear, was utilized and dissipated." (3)
- "Civilized man is prevented by the mores and ethics of society from responding to the emotion of fear in a muscular manner." (4)
- "Unable to express in action his reaction to this emotion, residual tension of somatic

muscles and altered function of visceral structures become the curse of civilized man. With long continued tension of somatic muscle comes structural alteration." (5)
- "This persistent residual tension and alteration in physiological function is reflected back through the afferent (sensory) components of the nervous system to give rise to the feelings of anxiety… the body's continued fear-response long after the cause of the fear has disappeared." (6)

According to Dr. Virgil Strang's text, "The body works on what may be called an energy-balance equation. That is, every bit of energy generated is expended – one way or another." (7) In other words, the human body can be likened to an electricity generator: the more talented an individual is, the more energy that develops within them to utilize that talent. However, when this equation becomes unbalanced (more energy being produced than is being used), other body systems must be utilized to dissipate the extra energy. Initially, neural facilitation mode is used by the body tissues and systems. According to Guyton…
- When an "input fiber contributes terminals to neurons… but not enough to cause excitation… discharge of these terminals makes these neurons more excitable to

signals arriving through the other incoming nerve fibers." Thus, "the neurons are said to be facilitated." (8)

So, in essence, when an individual encounters a situation where their talent could/should be used, the energy is developed automatically for that use. But, when that individual then fails to use this energy, a distortion occurs in the energy equation and an inverse reaction occurs in the dissipation. Facilitation mode then develops in the nervous system.

Muscle tissue is capable of conducting and thus, dissipating a greater amount of energy per unit of time than any other body system. By offering the least resistance to flow, muscle tissue balances the energy equation in situations involving extra energy.

As with primitive "fight or flight" mechanism, being about one's purpose for being creates an emotional feeling within us. And as Dr. Virgil Strang has stated in his lectures, "Every emotion has motion." (9) According to Guyton…
- "When large portions of the sympathetic nervous system discharge at the same time – that is, a mass discharge – this increases in many different ways the ability of the body to perform vigorous muscle activity." (10)

Thus, the individual is able to perform "far more strenuous physical activity than would otherwise be possible." (11)

- "The sympathetic system is especially strongly activated in many emotional states. For instance, in the state of rage, which is elicited mainly by stimulating the hypothalamus, signals are transmitted downward through the reticular formation and spinal cord to cause massive sympathetic discharge." (12)

Skeletal muscle, which can also be referred to as voluntary muscle, makes up 40% of the body's weight and mass and is under the control of educated intelligence. In other words, control of voluntary muscle involves a decisional process. Cardiac and smooth muscle, which can collectively be referred to as involuntary muscle, makes up 20% of the body's weight and mass and is under the control of Innate Intelligence. In other words, control of involuntary muscle involves an automatic or reflex response.

Both voluntary and involuntary muscle can balance the energy equation due to their minimal resistance to flow. However, because we have the ability to voluntarily override or suppress the voluntary muscle reactivity, the involuntary muscle ultimately serves as the pathway of least resistance for most of the energy dissipation.

In actuality, the above is somewhat of an oversimplification. Both voluntary and involuntary muscles dissipate the energy to some degree and there are gray areas differentiating the two.

For instance, let's assume that we have a situation where we have extra energy. In an effort to dissipate this extra energy, the anterior horn cell becomes facilitated. If we then voluntarily suppress this nerve root (e.g. voluntarily decide not to jump out of the way of an oncoming truck), the neuronal discharge can then get re-routed through the 2nd branch off the spinal nerve root (musculocutaneous/somatic branch) which supplies the 5th layer of the back musculature and controls movement of the spine, vertebra-by-vertebra. As Homewood says…

- "Even generalized muscular tension of a psychogenic nature superimposed upon the insult of irritation caused by other… forms of stress, could be conceived to be the 'straw that broke the camel's back' creating the localized subluxations in the regions of the spine under greatest total strain." (13)

Additionally, the neuronal discharge can get re-routed through fibers of the autonomic nervous

Weathering Accidental Enlightenment

system supplying viscera (internal organs) via involuntary muscle stimulation. In this manner, a reflex arc can be established which not only exacerbates the local subluxation but perpetuates it as well.

Addressing the local subluxation can provide short-term results for the patient but until the root cause is addressed, the problem will continue to return. In other words, until the patient learns to redirect their extra energy in a voluntary manner, either through pursuit of one's reason for being or through physical exertion (i.e. exercise), the subluxation is destined to persist.

Appendix D

Pre-History Thoughts & Musings

I am often asked if I have always been this up-beat and optimistic. The answer is a resounding "Yes!"… and "No." To give you a better idea of what I mean, here are three poems I wrote a long, long time ago. Enjoy!

Impossible

Nothing irks me greater
Than to hear a person say
It can't be done; it's impossible
Then simply walk away

Nothing is so hard to do
As that which "can't be done"
But just decide to "try" it
And half the battle's won

So put forth an extra effort
Give it all you've got
And you will be rewarded
For a battle so well fought

Weathering Accidental Enlightenment

Time

Time passes oh so quickly
Like vultures in pursuit
I wish sometimes to stop it
And nurture of its fruit

The good times seem so short in passing
The bad times oh so long!
It cuts you down to nothing
BANG! And then it's gone

Both of the previous two poems were written when I was only in 9th grade, as part of a Creative Writing class 'Poetry Project.' Both were also written during a time of quiet between my mother's battles with cancer and one year prior to her relapse and subsequent death.

This next poem was written while I was a sophomore in college and was inspired while listening to a song called Men Before The Mirror by Mark Isham. (1) It speaks to how we all sometimes busy ourselves in an effort to escape what it really sometimes feels like to be human.

Invisible Suppression

Busy schedules
Hectic days
No one to tell
Nothing to say
Keep moving on

Busy schedules
Hectic days
Hollow successes
Nothing to say

Keep moving on
Busy schedules
Hectic days
Silent torment
Nothing to say
Keep moving on
Busy schedules
Hectic days
Anguishing memories

Nothing to say
Keep moving on

Busy schedules
Hectic days
No time to feel

Weathering Accidental Enlightenment

Am I always this up-beat and optimistic? Most of the time, yes. Some might even accuse me of being annoyingly so. But, know this: it is a choice I make each and every day, a choice I have made for most of my life and a choice I intend to continue making!

Appendix E

Required Reading — 3 Plus One

iContractor 1 included an *Appendix A: Recommended Reading List* that was compiled from 60 of the books that were both personal favorites of mine and ones that I considered to have been the most useful to me on my journey up until that point in time. They were listed for the "serious student" who wished to take their learning to the next level.

At this time, I would like to boil that list down to only 3 plus one: the 3 from the prior list that I consider to have been *the* most influential to my thinking processes plus one more; the 4 books that I now consider to be "Required Reading" for everyone, everywhere.

Weathering Accidental Enlightenment

1.) **The Structure of Scientific Revolutions**
Thomas S. Kuhn
Second Edition, Enlarged
Chicago: The University of Chicago Press
Copyright 1962, 1970

What you see is NOT necessarily what you saw! Rather, what you expected to see GREATLY biases what your brain interprets itself as actually having seen, REGARDLESS of the existent reality.

First introduced to this book in a college philosophy class nearly 30 years ago, I would have to say that being introduced to this one work was, by far, the most important thing to happen to me during my undergraduate days at Saint Bonaventure University. This book forever changed how I viewed my "reality."

2.) **Man's Search For Meaning**
Viktor Frankl
Boston: Beacon Press
Copyright 1959, 2006

The first part of this book is absolutely terrible to read. It places the reader there with Viktor Frankl, right in the bowels of the concentration camps of the Holocaust. However, learning how Mr. Frankl not only survived, but actually thrived to some extent, by choosing his attitude on a daily, even moment-by-moment, basis offers a powerful lesson to us all for weathering the storms of life.

I first read this book while recovering from a surgical procedure back in 2009 and, much like when I read <u>Structure</u> (above), I was never the same after. My writing style and content changed dramatically. The first "HealthBeat" article I submitted to The Meadville Tribune (as part of a 10 year long collaborative effort by all of the local chiropractors) after this led to an offer to contribute a quarterly philosophy column of my own for their "Active for Life" supplement on an ongoing basis thereafter.

3.) **In Tune With The Infinite**
Ralph Waldo Trine
Copyright 1897

This is by far the best book I have found on New Thought and the Law of Attraction. What's more, this book takes the Law of Attraction right to the brink of the seemingly logical next step for me: the Law of Reflection.

The fact that Ralph Waldo Trine's writing style was very similar to my own made this book all the more enjoyable for me to read.

Weathering Accidental Enlightenment

4.) **Dark Night of the Soul**
St. John of the Cross
Written somewhere between 1578 and 1587
Translated and edited by E. Allison Peers
Dover Publications, Inc.
Copyright 2003

What makes this book so valuable to me is the manner in which it conveys the universality of the human condition. St. John of the Cross weathered more than his fair share of Dark Nights. And the manner in which he was able to describe, over 400 years ago, the exact same experience that I found myself in while writing The "Zero's Journey" left me feeling connected to something far bigger than myself, understood and not so all alone. In fact, in all of my years of study, only Dark Night of the Soul by St. John of the Cross and The Book of Job from the Old Testament come close to mirroring The "Zero's Journey" and both were first encountered by me AFTER having completed the vast majority of this manuscript. Only after describing my own Dark Night (Chapter 13) did I go back and read the descriptions offered by these two authors. Their words so poetically captured my own experience that I then went back and edited their quotes into this manuscript as well.

Permissions
(Listed in order of 1st appearance)

I would like to acknowledge the following publishers and individuals for permission to reprint the cited material:

- Excerpted from *The Structure of Scientific Revolutions* by Thomas S. Kuhn, © 1962, 1970 by The University of Chicago. All rights reserved. Published 1962. Second edition, enlarged, 1970. Reprinted with permission.
- Excerpted from *Awakening The Buddha Within: Tibetan Wisdom For The Western World* by Lama Surya Das, Random House, Inc. Reprinted with permission.
- Quote of Wil Garcia used by permission from George Melton, author of *Beyond Aids: A Journey Into Healing* and *A Ride On The Cosmic Slingshot*.
- Excerpted from *THE WORLD ACCORDING TO MISTER ROGERS: Important Things to Remember* by Fred Rogers. Published by Hachette Book Group, Inc., 237 Park Ave, New York, NY 10017. Reprinted with permission.
- From *"Man's Search for Meaning"* by Viktor E. Frankl. Copyright © 1959, 1962,

1984, 1992 by Viktor E. Frankl. Reprinted by permission of Beacon Press, Boston.
- Excerpted from *The Alchemist* by Paulo Coelho and translated by Alan R. Clarke. © 1993, Harper Collins Publishers. Reprinted with permission.
- Excerpted from *The Next Step* by Arthur Jones. Used with permission courtesy of http://www.arthurjonesexercise.com/
- Jon D. Ketcham, interviewed by the author.
- Quote of Anthony Robbins used by permission from Robbins Research International. Inc.
- Stephen Duncanson, interviewed by the author.
- © Ayya Khema, 1997. Reprinted from *Who Is My Self: A Guide to Buddhist Meditation* with permission from Wisdom Publications, 199 Elm Street, Somerville, MA 02144 USA. www.wisdompubs.org
- © Ayya Khema, 2000. Reprinted from *When the Iron Eagle Flies: Buddhism for the West* with permission from Wisdom Publications, 199 Elm Street, Somerville, MA 02144 USA. www.wisdompubs.org
- Excerpted from *The Soul of Money* by Lynne Twist, W.W. Norton & Company. Reprinted with permission.

- Excerpted from *The Riches Within* by John F. Demartini, © 2008, Hay House, Inc., Carlsbad, CA. Reprinted with permission.
- Excerpted from Denis Waitley Newsletter, August 21, 2012, Issue 215. Reprinted with permission.
- Excerpted from *Being The Present* by Pilar Stella & Cynthia Aliza Blake, Morgan James Publishing. Reprinted with permission.
- Excerpted from *Anatomy of an Illness* by Norman Cousins, W.W. Norton & Company. Reprinted by permission.
- Excerpted from *In Search Of The Invisible Forces* by George Addair. Reprinted with permission from The Omega Vector.
- Excerpted from *Are You The Doctor, Doctor?* by F. H. Barge. Reprinted with permission from Patty Barge.
- Jacob Nordby, interviewed by the author.
- Excerpted from Eckhart Tolle's October 2011 newsletter. Reprinted with permission.
- Excerpted from *Getting Well Again* by O. Carl Simonton, M.D., Stephanie Matthews-Simonton and James L. Creighton, Random House, Inc. Reprinted with permission.
- Excerpted from *On Death and Dying* by Elisabeth Kübler-Ross, M.D., Simon & Schuster, Inc. Reprinted with permission.

Weathering Accidental Enlightenment

- Excerpted from *The Dark Night of the Soul* by Gerald G. May, M.D. © 2004, Harper Collins Publishers. Reprinted with permission.
- Excerpted from Neale Donald Walsch's newsletter, author of *Conversations with God*. Reprinted with permission.
- Ram Dass quote used by permission from Ram Dass / Love Serve Remember Foundation – For more information go to RamDass.org
- Excerpted from *Into the Wind* by Jake Ducey. Reprinted with permission from the author.
- Excerpted from *Essential Principles of Chiropractic* by Virgil V. Strang. Reprinted with permission from Dr. Victor Strang.
- Excerpted from *Textbook of Medical Physiology* by Arthur C. Guyton, pp. 501 and 676, Eighth Edition, Copyright Elsevier 1991. Reprinted with permission.

Sources

A Couple Quick Notes Pertaining To The Quotes
(1) www.GoodReads.com, Charles Spurgeon

Preface
(1) Brian Tracy Quote of the Day, 10/05/2012, Appius Claudius Caecus
(2) Bartlett's Familiar Quotations, John Bartlett p. 589

Introduction

Reflector Vector – Deconstructing the "Law of Attraction"
(1) www.Merriam-Webster.com, paradigm
(2) The Structure of Scientific Revolutions, Thomas Kuhn p. 23
(3) The Structure of Scientific Revolutions, Thomas Kuhn pp. 67-68
(4) The Structure of Scientific Revolutions, Thomas Kuhn p. 85
(5) The Structure of Scientific Revolutions, Thomas Kuhn p. 68
(6) Proceedings of the Third Biennial Convention of the Amalgamated Clothing Workers of America, p. 53 (1918); Wikiquote, Mohandas Karamchand Gandhi

Weathering Accidental Enlightenment

(7) <u>In Tune With The Infinite</u>, Ralph Waldo Trine (1897)
(8) <u>The Science of Getting Rich</u>, Wallace Wattles (1910)
(9) <u>The Master Key System</u>, Charles Haanel (1912)
(10) <u>Think And Grow Rich</u>, Napoleon Hill (1937)
(11) <u>The Secret</u>, Rhonda Byrne (2006)
(12) <u>iContractor 1</u>, Dr. Jon M. Ketcham (2012)
(13) <u>Bible</u>, Luke 17:21
(14) <u>Bible</u>, Psalm 23
(15) The Bhagavad-Gita, The Eighteenth Teaching verse 61
(16) The Bhagavad-Gita, The Eighteenth Teaching verse 78
(17) <u>Awakening The Buddha Within</u>, Lama Surya Das pp. 70 & 20
(18) <u>Bartlett's Familiar Quotations</u>, John Bartlett p. 659
(19) <u>Bible</u>, Genesis 1:27
(20) <u>Bible</u>, John 8:12
(21) <u>Bible</u>, John 10:30
(22) <u>iContractor 1</u>, Dr. Jon M. Ketcham p. 10
(23) <u>Awakening The Buddha Within</u>, Lama Surya Das pp. 14-15
(24) <u>The Game of Life and How To Play It</u>, Florence Scovel Shinn p. 39

(25) Bible, Genesis 1:27
(26) Bible, Psalm 23
(27) The Divine Arsonist, Jacob Nordby p. 288
(28) Bible, Mark 11:24

StairWELL to Success... Steps and More Steps
(1) Tao Te Ching, Lao Tzu section 71
(2) www.BrainyQuote.com, Benjamin Franklin Quotes; Poor Richard's Almanac, Benjamin Franklin
(3) Wikipedia "Know Thyself": Isha Schwaller De Lubicz, Lucie Lamy, Her-Bak: Egyptian Initiate., (Inner Traditions International, 1978)
(4) Wikipedia "Know Thyself": Socrates use of 'Know thyself' in Philebus (48c) http://www.perseus.tufts.edu/hopper/text?doc=Plat.+Phileb.+48c&fromdoc=Perseus:text:1999.01.0174
(5) www.GoodReads.com, Aristotle; http://lifechangequotes.com
(6) Bible, Genesis 1:27
(7) www.BrainyQuote.com, Pierre Teilhard de Chardin Quotes
(8) The Book of Positive Quotations, John Cook p. 44
(9) Brian Tracy Quote of the Day, 07/16/2012, Thomas Paine
(10) Bible, Genesis 1:27

Weathering Accidental Enlightenment

(11) www.BrainyQuote.com, Lucille Ball Quotes; Bob Proctor's Insight of the Day, 09/20/2012, Lucille Ball

(12) VH-1 Behind the Music – Meatloaf (1998)

(13) www.LivingLifeFully.com/acceptance.htm, Wil Garcia

(14) Back To School (DVD)

(15) iContractor 1, Dr. Jon M. Ketcham p. 55

(16) Brian Tracy Quote of the Day, 08/26/2012, J.C. Penney

(17) www.BrainyQuote.com, Michelangelo Quotes; www.ThinkExist.com, Michelangelo

(18) Bartlett's Familiar Quotations, John Bartlett p. 129

(19) The World According to Mister Rogers: Important Things to Remember, Fred Rogers p. 19, published by Hachette Book Group, Inc.

(20) www.BrainyQuote.com, Plutarch Quotes

(21) www.ThinkExist.com, Charlie Chaplin quotes; Bob Proctor's Insight of the Day, 06/11/2012, Charlie Chaplin

(22) iContractor 1, Dr. Jon M. Ketcham p. 46

(23) The Success Principles, Jack Canfield pp. 93-94

Finding Your AFFLATUS... Constructing Your Magnificent "Why"

(1) <u>Webster's New Universal Unabridged Dictionary</u>, 1996 edition, p. 34
(2) <u>The Princeton Encyclopedia Of Poetry & Poetics</u>, Fourth Edition p. 13
(3) <u>The Princeton Encyclopedia Of Poetry & Poetics</u>, Fourth Edition p. 709
(4) <u>iContractor 1</u>, Dr. Jon M. Ketcham p. 11
(5) <u>Bible</u>, Matthew 6:21
(6) <u>Bible</u>, Proverbs 17:8
(7) <u>Bible</u>, Proverbs 18:16
(8) <u>Bible</u>, 1 Timothy 4:14
(9) <u>Bartlett's Familiar Quotations</u>, John Bartlett p. 765
(10) <u>The Game of Life and How To Play It</u>, Florence Scovel Shinn p. 7
(11) <u>Man's Search For Meaning</u>, Viktor Frankl p. 109 [From "Man's Search for Meaning" by Viktor E. Frankl. Copyright © 1959, 1962, 1984, 1992 by Viktor E. Frankl. Reprinted by permission of Beacon Press, Boston.]
(12) <u>The Alchemist</u>, Paulo Coelho p. 22 [From "The Alchemist" by Paulo Coelho and translated by Alan R. Clarke. © 1993, Harper Collins Publishers.]
(13) <u>Wall-E</u> (DVD)

Weathering Accidental Enlightenment

(14) Your Achievement Newsletter September 26, 2012, Vincent van Gogh
(15) <u>Acres of Diamonds</u>, Russell H. Conwell p. 57
(16) <u>The Book of Positive Quotations</u>, John Cook p. 474
(17) <u>The Bhagavad-Gita</u>, The Eighteenth Teaching verse 47
(18) <u>The Prophet</u>, Kahlil Gibran p. 35
(19) <u>Bible</u>, Proverbs 17:22
(20) <u>The Book of Positive Quotations</u>, John Cook p. 291
(21) <u>iContractor 1</u>, Dr. Jon M. Ketcham p. 67
(22) <u>IronMan Magazine</u>, July 1971, Vol. 30 No.5, "The Next Step" by Arthur Jones. Used with permission courtesy of http://www.arthurjonesexercise.com/
(23) <u>In Tune With The Infinite</u>, Ralph Waldo Trine p. 51
(24) <u>The Dark Night Of The Soul</u>, Saint John of the Cross
(25) <u>The Alchemist</u>, Paulo Coelho p. 111 [From "The Alchemist" by Paulo Coelho and translated by Alan R. Clarke. © 1993, Harper Collins Publishers.]
(26) Excerpt from <u>The Dark Night Of The Soul</u> (poem), Saint John of the Cross
(27) <u>Think And Grow Rich</u>, Napoleon Hill p. 5

The Zero's Journey

(28) *Awakening The Buddha Within*, Lama Surya Das p.124
(29) Per Jonny Ketcham, age 15, July 31, 2010
(30) *Fat Albert*, Bill Cosby (TV Show)
(31) *Bible*, Proverbs 20:30
(32) *Man's Search For Meaning*, Viktor Frankl p. 76
(33) *Finding Your Purpose, Getting A Life*, Dr. Jon M. Ketcham
(34) *The Divine Arsonist*, Jacob Nordby p. 95
(35) *Bible*, Mark 11:24
(36) *The Book of Positive Quotations*, John Cook p. 142
(37) *Bible*, Luke 17:21
(38) *The Book of Positive Quotations*, John Cook p. 371
(39) www.ThinkExist.com, Oliver Wendell Holmes
(40) Neale Donald Walsch, daily e-mail newsletter, 11/29/2011, Leonardo da Vinci

Attitude
(1) *The Book of Positive Quotations*, John Cook p. 55
(2) www.scenicwonders.com/california-redwood-trees/
(3) www.drpaulose.com/spirituality/tree-of-life-in-bahrain-desert-faith-in-adversity

Weathering Accidental Enlightenment

(4) www.BrainyQuote.com, Khalil Gibran Quotes
(5) Bartlett's Familiar Quotations, John Bartlett p. 454
(6) Oprah's Lifeclass on OWN Network, 10/28/2012
(7) Man's Search For Meaning, Viktor Frankl p. 66 [From "Man's Search for Meaning" by Viktor E. Frankl. Copyright © 1959, 1962, 1984, 1992 by Viktor E. Frankl. Reprinted by permission of Beacon Press, Boston.]
(8) Bob Proctor's Insight of the Day, 7/31/2012, Viktor Frankl
(9) www.Pachamama.org/about/mission-and-vision; www.GoodReads.com, Albert Einstein
(10) The Book of Positive Quotations, John Cook p. 35

Faith

(1) The Book of Positive Quotations, John Cook p. 122
(2) How To Become A Millionaire!, John Earl Shoaff (CD – track 6 of 7)
(3) The Book of Positive Quotations, John Cook p. 118
(4) Bible, Hebrews 11:1
(5) Think And Grow Rich, Napoleon Hill p. 19
(6) The Art of War, Sun Tzu p. 134

(7) The Art of War, Sun Tzu p. 137
(8) The Art of War, Sun Tzu p. 139
(9) Tao Te Ching, Lao Tzu Section 49
(10) Wikipedia: Wilma Rudolph
(11) Bob Proctor's Insight of the Day, 7/5/2012, Wilma Rudolph
(12) Brian Tracy's Quote of the Day, 7/1/2012, Wilma Rudolph
(13) www.BrainyQuote.com, Muhammad Ali Quotes
(14) www.BrainyQuote.com, Jack Dempsey Quotes; Bill Hinbern Newsletter, 7/5/2012;
(15) iContractor 1, Dr. Jon M. Ketcham p. 46
(16) www.ThinkExist.com, Anthony Robbins quotes; www.TonyRobbins.com
(17) Live Full And Die Empty, Les Brown (DVD); also per discussion with Stephen Duncanson
(18) Who Is My Self?: A Guide To Buddhist Meditation, Ayya Khema p. 82
(19) When The Iron Eagle Flies: Buddhism for the West, Ayya Khema p. 90
(20) www.GoodReads.com, Rumi
(21) Bible, II Corinthians 5:7
(22) Bible, Joel 2:25-26

Weathering Accidental Enlightenment

Financial Consciousness
(1) The Book of Positive Quotations, John Cook p. 369
(2) Bible, 1 Timothy 6:10
(3) Acres of Diamonds, Russell H. Conwell pp. 26-27
(4) Bible, Psalm 23
(5) Acres of Diamonds, Russell H. Conwell p. 45
(6) The Soul of Money, Lynne Twist pp. 103-104
(7) The Book of Positive Quotations, John Cook p. 158
(8) Bartlett's Familiar Quotations, John Bartlett p. 457
(9) Bartlett's Familiar Quotations, John Bartlett p. 454
(10) Bible, Matthew 25:29
(11) Bible, Luke, 19:26
(12) Tao Te Ching, Lao Tzu Section 44
(13) The Riches Within, Dr. John F. Demartini p. 64
(14) Denis Waitley Newsletter, August 21, 2012 Issue 215
(15) Neale Donald Walsch, daily e-mail newsletter, 01/23/2012, Robert Collier

Laughter
  (1) <u>BEing the Present: 101 Ways to Inspire Living and Giving</u>, Pilar Stella, Cynthia Aliza Blake p. 153
  (2) <u>Bartlett's Familiar Quotations</u>, John Bartlett p. 356
  (3) <u>Anatomy of an Illness</u>, Norman Cousins p. 39
  (4) <u>www.BrainyQuote.com</u>, William James Quotes
  (5) <u>www.QuoteIdea.com</u>, Viktor Frankl Quotes
  (6) <u>www.BrainyQuote.com</u>, Charlie Chaplin Quotes
  (7) <u>Bartlett's Familiar Quotations</u>, John Bartlett p. 562
  (8) <u>www.BrainyQuote.com</u>, Voltaire Quotes
  (9) <u>www.BrainyQuote.com</u>, Elbert Hubbard Quotes
  (10) <u>Monster's, Inc.</u> (DVD)

Allowing
  (1) <u>The Book of Positive Quotations</u>, John Cook p. 535
  (2) <u>Man's Search For Meaning</u>, Viktor Frankl p. 122 [From "Man's Search for Meaning" by Viktor E. Frankl. Copyright © 1959, 1962, 1984, 1992 by Viktor E. Frankl. Reprinted by permission of Beacon Press, Boston.]

Weathering Accidental Enlightenment

(3) The Book of Positive Quotations, John Cook p. 186
(4) The Power of Now, Eckhart Tolle
(5) iContractor 1, Dr. Jon M. Ketcham pp. 34-35
(6) iContractor 1, Dr. Jon M. Ketcham p. 62
(7) The Birds of Killingworth, Henry Wadsworth Longfellow (1915)

Thanksgiving
(1) Creative Mind, Ernest Holmes p. 38
(2) www.ThinkExist.com, George Bernard Shaw quotes; www.QuotesDaddy.com
(3) www.SearchQuotes.com, Bertrand Russell; www.QuotationsBook.com
(4) Bartlett's Familiar Quotations, John Bartlett p. 282
(5) www.BrainyQuote.com, Desiderius Erasmus Quotes
(6) Bible, 1 Thessalonians 5:18-19
(7) The Book of Positive Quotations, John Cook p. 53
(8) www.BrainyQuote.com, Henri Matisse Quotes

U.S.P. "Unique Selling Proposition"
(1) The Book of Positive Quotations, John Cook p. 172
(2) Wikipedia "Molting"

(3) The Book of Positive Quotations, John Cook p. 327
(4) Live Full And Die Empty (DVD)
(5) Change Your Brain, Change Your Life, Daniel G. Amen, M.D.
(6) Per lecture at Experts Industry Association Conference 2011
(7) Live Full And Die Empty (DVD)
(8) In Search Of The Invisible Forces, George Addair p. 30
(9) In Search Of The Invisible Forces, George Addair p. 30
(10) In Tune With The Infinite, Ralph Waldo Trine p. 75
(11) Are You The Doctor, Doctor?, F.H. Barge p. 2
(12) Bartlett's Familiar Quotations, John Bartlett p. 455
(13) The Book of Positive Quotations, John Cook p. 170
(14) www.BlessedAreTheWeird.com

Service
(1) Wikiquote — Charles Dickens from Our Mutual Friend
(2) Bible, Matthew 25:14-30
(3) Bible, Luke 19:12-28
(4) The Book of Positive Quotations, John Cook p. 79

Weathering Accidental Enlightenment

(5) The Book of Positive Quotations, John Cook p. 79
(6) www.BrainyQuote.com, Dalai Lama Quotes
(7) Bartlett's Familiar Quotations, John Bartlett p. 589
(8) Walden, Henry David Thoreau p. 22
(9) www.QuoteWorld.org, Johann Wolfgang von Goethe; www.aquotes.net
(10) Excerpt from "Humpty Dumpty" Nursery Rhyme
(11) Attributed to John Bunyan (1628-1688); www.Goodreads.com, John Bunyan Quotes
(12) The Book of Positive Quotations, John Cook p. 79

Walking in Silence — Solitary Refinement

(1) www.BrainyQuote.com, John Bunyan Quotes
(2) Bible, Matthew 6:7-8
(3) Bible, Romans 8:28
(4) Quran, 18:23-24
(5) The Book of Positive Quotations, John Cook p. 219
(6) www.SelfGrowth.com, Self-Improvement and Personal Growth Weekly Newsletter, Issue #788, Week of October 14-15, 2013, Virgil quote
(7) The Book of Positive Quotations, John Cook p. 122

Weathering the "Dark Nights" - A Tale of Two Survivors

(1) Bartlett's Familiar Quotations, John Bartlett p. 746
(2) Wikipedia "Dark Night of the Soul"
(3) www.BrainyQuote.com, Alexis de Tocqueville Quotes
(4) Man's Search For Meaning, Viktor Frankl p. 70 [From "Man's Search for Meaning" by Viktor E. Frankl. Copyright © 1959, 1962, 1984, 1992 by Viktor E. Frankl. Reprinted by permission of Beacon Press, Boston.]
(5) Man's Search For Meaning, Viktor Frankl p. 70 [From "Man's Search for Meaning" by Viktor E. Frankl. Copyright © 1959, 1962, 1984, 1992 by Viktor E. Frankl. Reprinted by permission of Beacon Press, Boston.]
(6) Dark Night of the Soul, St. John of the Cross, Book II Chapter VI
(7) Ron White's Newsletter, August 15, 2012 Issue 179, Oliver Wendell Holmes
(8) Bible, Mark 15:34
(9) Bible, Matthew 27:46
(10) Bible, Psalm 22:1
(11) Eckhart Tolle Newsletter, October 2011

Weathering Accidental Enlightenment

(12) <u>Man's Search For Meaning</u>, Viktor Frankl pp. 71-72, 74 [From "Man's Search for Meaning" by Viktor E. Frankl. Copyright © 1959, 1962, 1984, 1992 by Viktor E. Frankl. Reprinted by permission of Beacon Press, Boston.]

(13) <u>Bible</u>, Galatians 6:9

(14) <u>Bible</u>, James 1:12

(15) <u>The Book of Positive Quotations</u>, John Cook p. 287

(16) <u>Man's Search For Meaning</u>, Viktor Frankl p. 75 [From "Man's Search for Meaning" by Viktor E. Frankl. Copyright © 1959, 1962, 1984, 1992 by Viktor E. Frankl. Reprinted by permission of Beacon Press, Boston.]

(17) <u>Getting Well Again</u>, O. Carl Simonton, M.D., Stephanie Matthews-Simonton, James L. Creighton p. 54

(18) <u>Getting Well Again</u>, O. Carl Simonton, M.D., Stephanie Matthews-Simonton, James L. Creighton p. 10

(19) <u>On Death and Dying</u>, Elisabeth Kübler-Ross, M.D. p. 149

(20) <u>www.BrainyQuote.com</u>, Helen Keller Quotes

(21) <u>Bartlett's Familiar Quotations</u>, John Bartlett p. 363

(22) <u>www.BrainyQuote.com</u>, Morris West Quotes

(23) www.BrainyQuote.com, Pliny the Elder Quotes

The Coming of the Dawn
(1) <u>Sand and Foam</u>, Kahlil Gibran
(2) WikiQuote <u>http://en.wikiquote.org/wiki/Niels_Bohr</u> , as quoted by Edward Teller in <u>Dr. Edward Teller's Magnificent Obsession</u> by Richard Coughlan in LIFE magazine (6 September 1954) p. 62
(3) <u>iContractor 1</u>, Dr. Jon M. Ketcham p. 71
(4) <u>Bible</u>, Ephesians 2:8-9
(5) <u>The Dark Night of the Soul</u>, Gerald G. May, M.D. p. 180 [From "The Dark Night of the Soul" by Gerald G. May, M.D. © 2004, Harper Collins Publishers.]
(6) Neale Donald Walsch, daily e-mail newsletter, 4/21/2011
(7) <u>The Book of Positive Quotations</u>, John Cook p. 386
(8) <u>Bible</u>, Genesis 1:27
(9) Per Lisa Ketcham, October 21, 2013 (6 months AFTER finding employment at a busy medical practice)
(10) www.BrainyQuote.com, Paul Valery Quotes

Weathering Accidental Enlightenment

The "Zero's Journey"
 (1) Bible, Job 30:19
 (2) The Prophet, Kahlil Gibran p. 8
 (3) Bartlett's Familiar Quotations, John Bartlett p. 589
 (4) Dark Night of the Soul, St. John of the Cross, Book II Chapter VI
 (5) The Works of Mencius, Book VI Kâo Tsze Part II Section XV 2.
 (6) The Prophet, Kahlil Gibran pp. 11 & 61
 (7) Tao Te Ching, Lao Tzu Section 52
 (8) Bible, Job 30:19
 (9) Wikipedia "Bhagwan Shree Rajneesh (Osho)"
 (10) www.ThinkExist.com, Lao Tzu quotes
 (11) Dark Night of the Soul, St. John of the Cross, Book II Chapter II
 (12) The Dark Night of the Soul, Gerald G. May, M.D. p. 167 [From "The Dark Night of the Soul" by Gerald G. May, M.D. © 2004, Harper Collins Publishers.]
 (13) Bible, Genesis 1:27
 (14) Ram Dass / Love Serve Remember Foundation – For more information go to RamDass.org
 (15) Neale Donald Walsch, daily e-mail newsletter, 11/29/2013
 (16) IslamicArtDB.com, Imam Ali ibn-Abi-Talib

(17) www.BrainyQuote.com, Emily Dickinson Quotes
(18) The Book of Positive Quotations, John Cook p. 256
(19) The Christian Sentinel or Soldiers' Magazine (1867), "No Garden without a Sepulchre" p. 218 [inclusive of quote from Bible, Job 14:1]
(20) Sand and Foam, Kahlil Gibran

Afterward: Crossing the "Fault Line"
(1) In Search Of The Invisible Forces, George Addair p. 24
(2) iContractor 1, Dr. Jon M. Ketcham p. 1
(3) Bible, Job

Epilogue: 20¢ worth of Philosophy 1 Year Later
(1) Bartlett's Familiar Quotations, John Bartlett p. 364
(2) www.BrainyQuote.com, Charles Kingsley Quotes
(3) www.BrainyQuote.com, Henry David Thoreau Quotes
(4) Into The Wind, Jake Ducey p. 24
(5) To a Mouse, Robert Burns
(6) The Book of Positive Quotations, John Cook p. 114
(7) The Book of Positive Quotations, John Cook p. 85

Weathering Accidental Enlightenment

About The Author
(1) Journals of Ralph Waldo Emerson Volume IV 1820 -1872, Ralph Waldo Emerson p. 78

Appendix B: The "Safety Pin Cycle" – revisited
  (1) Chiropractic Textbook, Vol. XIV, R.W. Stephenson p. 9
  (2) Unlimited Riches, Mark Victor Hansen, (Audio Cassette Program, Tape 1A)

Appendix C: Being About One's Purpose For Being
  (1) Opening phrase of the soliloquy from Hamlet, William Shakespeare
  (2) The Neurodynamics of the Vertebral Subluxation, A.E. Homewood p. 96
  (3) The Neurodynamics of the Vertebral Subluxation, A.E. Homewood p. 96
  (4) The Neurodynamics of the Vertebral Subluxation, A.E. Homewood p. 96
  (5) The Neurodynamics of the Vertebral Subluxation, A.E. Homewood p. 96
  (6) The Neurodynamics of the Vertebral Subluxation, A.E. Homewood p. 96
  (7) Essential Principles of Chiropractic, Virgil V. Strang p. 147
  (8) Textbook of Medical Physiology, Eighth Edition, Arthur C. Guyton, Chapter 46 – Sensory Receptors; Neuronal Circuits for

Processing Information, p. 501, Copyright Elsevier 1991.
(9) Per Dr. Strang's lectures during 9th Trimester Philosophy class 1996
(10) <u>Textbook of Medical Physiology</u>, Eighth Edition, Arthur C. Guyton, Chapter 60 – The Autonomic Nervous System; The Adrenal Medulla, p. 676, Copyright Elsevier 1991.
(11) <u>Textbook of Medical Physiology</u>, Eighth Edition, Arthur C. Guyton, Chapter 60 – The Autonomic Nervous System; The Adrenal Medulla, p. 676, Copyright Elsevier 1991.
(12) <u>Textbook of Medical Physiology</u>, Eighth Edition, Arthur C. Guyton, Chapter 60 – The Autonomic Nervous System; The Adrenal Medulla, p. 676, Copyright Elsevier 1991.
(13) <u>The Neurodynamics of the Vertebral Subluxation</u>, A.E. Homewood p. 94

Appendix D: Pre-History Thoughts & Musings
(1) <u>Vapor Drawings</u>, Mark Isham (cd)

Weathering Accidental Enlightenment

Bibliography

Addair, George. *In Search of The Invisible Forces.* Phoenix: Vector, MCMLCV.

Ali, Muhammad. *BrainyQuote.com.* Xplore Inc. 2013. http://www.brainyquote.com/quotes/authors/m/muhammad_ali.html (accessed March 3, 2013).

Amen, Dr. Daniel. "per lecture at Experts Industry Association Conference." Santa Clara, CA, 2011.

Aristotle. *GoodReads.com.* 2013. http://www.goodreads.com/quotes/3102-knowing-yourself-is-the-beginning-of-all-wisdom (accessed March 5, 2013).

Back To School. Produced by Metro Goldwyn Mayer. 1986.

Ball, Lucille. *BrainyQuote.com.* Xplore, Inc. 2013. http://www.brainyquote.com/quotes/authors/l/lucille_ball.html (accessed March 6, 2013).

Barge, F. H. *Are You The Doctor, Doctor?* Third Edition. Vol. IV. Eldridge, IA: Bawden Printing, Inc., 1984.

Bartlett, John. *Bartlett's Familiar Quotations.* Seventeenth Edition. New York, NY: Little, Brown and Company, 2002.

Beecher, Reverend Henry Ward. "No Garden without a Sepulchre." *The Christian Sentinel or Soldiers' Magazine*, 1867: 218.

BlessedAreTheWierd.com. 2013. http://www.blessedarethewierd.com (accessed March 4, 2013).

Live Full And Die Empty. Produced by Seminars On DVD (www.seminarsonDVD.com). Performed by Les Brown. 2006.

Bunyan, John. *BrainyQuote.com.* Xplore Inc. 2014. http://www.brainyquote.com/quotes/quotes/j/johnbunyan107371.html (accessed February 24, 2014).

Weathering Accidental Enlightenment

—. *Goodreads.com.* 2014. http://www.goodreads.com/author/quotes/16244.John_Bunyan (accessed February 24, 2014).

Burns, Robert. *To a Mouse.* 1785.

Byrne, Rhonda. *The Secret.* New York: Atria Books (A Division of Simon & Schuster, Inc.), 2006.

Caecus, Appius Claudius. "Brian Tracy Quote of the Day." *daily e-mail newsletter.* October 5, 2012.

Canfield, Jack. *The Success Principles.* New York: Harper Collins Publishers, 2005.

Chaplin, Charlie. *BrainyQuote.com.* Xplore Inc. 2013. http://www.brainyquote.com/quotes/authors/c/charlie_chaplin.html (accessed February 25, 2013).

—. *ThinkExist.com.* 2013. http://thinkexist.com/quotation/you-have-to-believe-in-yourself-that-s-the-secret/365501.html (accessed March 3, 2013).

Chardin, Pierre Teilhard de. *BrainyQuote.com.* Xplore Inc. 2013. http://www.brainyquote.com/quotes/authors/p/pierre_teilhard_de_chardi.html (accessed February 25, 2013).

Coelho, Paulo. *The Alchemist.* Translated by Alan R. Clarke. New York: Harper One, 1993.

Collier, Robert. "Neale Donald Walsch "I Believe God Wants You To Know"." *daily e-mail newsletter.* January 23, 2012.

Conwell, Russell H. *Acres Of Diamonds.* Fleming H. Revell edition (1960); Jove edition (1978). New York: Jove Books via The Berkley Publishing Group, 1988.

Cook, John. *The Book Of Positive Quotations.* Minneapolis, Minnesota: Fairview Press, 1997.

Fat Albert and the Cosby Kids. Produced by Filmation. Performed by Bill Cosby. unknown.

Cousins, Norman. *Anatomy of an Illness as Perceived by the Patient.* New York: W. W. Norton & Company, Inc., 1979.

Cross, Saint John of the. *The Dark Night of the Soul.* 1578.
Cross, St. John of the. *Dark Night of the Soul.* Translated by E. Allison Peers.
Daniel G. Amen, M.D. *Change Your Brain, Change Your Life.* New York: Three Rivers Press - A Member of the Crown Publishing Group, 1998.
Das, Lama Surya. *Awakening The Buddha Within.* New York: Broadway Books, 1997.
Dass, Ram. *Love Serve Remember Foundation.* http://www.RamDass.org (accessed December 16, 2013).
Demartini, Dr. John F. *The Riches Within.* Carlsbad, CA: Hay House, Inc., 2008.
Dempsey, Jack. *BrainyQuote.com.* Xplore Inc. 2013. http://www.brainyquote.com/quotes/authors/j/jack_dempsey.html (accessed February 25, 2013).
Dickens, Charles. *Wikiquote.* http://en.wikiquote.org/wiki/Charles_Dickens (accessed November 20, 2013).
Dickinson, Emily. *BrainyQuote.com.* Xplore Inc. 2014. http://www.brainyquote.com/quotes/quotes/e/emilydicki132723.html (accessed January 3, 2014).
Ducey, Jake. *Into The Wind.* Cardiff, CA: Waterfront Publishing, 2013.
Einstein, Albert. *The Pachamama Alliance.* http://www.pachamama.org/about/mission-and-vision (accessed March 5, 2013).
Elder, Pliny the. *BrainyQuote.com.* Xplore Inc. 2013. http://www.brainyquote.com/quotes/quotes/p/plinytheel120362.html (accessed November 18, 2013).
Emerson, Ralph Waldo. *Journals Of Ralph Waldo Emerson Volume IV 1820-1872.* Haughton Mifflin Company - The Riverside Press Company, 1910.
Erasmus, Desiderius. *BrainyQuote.com.* Xplore Inc. 2013. http://www.brainyquote.com/quotes/authors/d/desiderius_erasmus.html (accessed March 3, 2013).

Weathering Accidental Enlightenment

Frankl, Viktor. "Bob Proctor's Insight of the Day." *daily e-mail newsletter.* July 31, 2012.

—. *Man's Search For Meaning.* Boston: Beacon Press, 1959; 2006.

—. *QuoteIdea.com.* 2013. http://www.quoteidea.com/authors/viktor-frankl-quotes (accessed February 25, 2013).

Franklin, Benjamin. *BrainyQuote.com.* Xplore Inc. 2013. http://www.brainyquote.com/quotes/authors/b/benjamin_franklin_3.html (accessed February 25, 2013).

Garcia, Wil. *LivingLifeFully.com.* 2013. http://www.livinglifefully.com/acceptance.htm (accessed March 9, 2013).

Gibran, Kahlil. *Sand and Foam.* 1926.

—. *The Prophet.* Alfred A. Knopf, 1923.

Gibran, Khalil. *BrainyQuote.com.* Xplore Inc. 2013. http://www.brainyquote.com./quotes/authors/k/khalil_gibran.html (accessed February 25, 2013).

Goethe, Johann Wolfgang von. *QuoteWorld.org.* 2013. http://www.quoteworld.org/quotes/5588 (accessed March 5, 2013).

Gogh, Vincent van. "Your Achievement Newsletter." *weekly e-mail newsletter from newsletter@yoursuccessstore.com.* September 26, 2012.

Guyton, Arthur C. *Textbook of Medical Physiology.* Eighth Edition. Philadelphia: W.B. Saunders Company, 1991.

Haanel, Charles. *The Master Key System.* written in 1912 and published in 1916. Public Domain, 1916.

Hansen, Mark Victor. *Unlimited Riches.* 1995.

Hill, Napoleon. *Think And Grow Rich.* New York: Fawcett Crest Edition, 1960.

Holmes, Ernest. *Creative Mind.* 1919.

Holmes, Oliver Wendell. "Ron White's Newsletter." *bi-weekly e-mail newsletter.* no. 179. August 15, 2012.

—. *ThinkExist.com.* 2014. http://thinkexist.com/quotation/the_greatest_tragedy_in_a

merica_is_not_the/325023.html (accessed February 12, 2014).

Holy Bible.

Homewood, A. E. *The Neurodynamics of the Vertebral Subluxation.* Third Edition, Third Printing 1981. 1962.

Hubbard, Elbert. *BrainyQuote.com.* Xplore Inc. 2013. http://www.brainyquote.com/quotes/authors/e/elbert_hubbard.html (accessed February 25, 2013).

Humpty Dumpty.

ibn-Abi-Talib, Ali. *IslamicArtDB.com.* 2014. http://islamicartdb.com/nothing-should-own-you/ (accessed February 17, 2014).

Isham, Mark. "Men Before The Mirror." *Vapor Drawings.* 1983.

James, William. *BrainyQuote.com.* Xplore Inc. 2013. http://www.brainyquote.com/quotes/authors/w/william_james_2.html (accessed February 25, 2013).

Jones, Arthur. *IronMan Magazine*, July 1971.

Keller, Helen. *BrainyQuote.com.* Xplore Inc. 2013. http://www.brainyquote.com/quotes/authors/h/helen_keller.html (accessed March 3, 2013).

Ketcham, Dr. Jon M. *iContractor 1... Constructing Your Perfect Life by Remodeling YOU from the Inside-Out!* New York: Morgan James Publishing, 2012.

—. "Finding Your Purpose, Getting A Life." *The Meadville Tribune, "Active for Life" supplement*, 2010.

Ketcham, Jonny. "per talking with Jonny Ketcham; my son, age 15." Meadville, PA, July 31, 2010.

Khema, Ayya. *When The Iron Eagle Flies: Buddhism for the West.* Somerville, MA: Wisdom Publications, 1991.

—. *Who Is My Self?: A Guide To Buddhist Meditation.* Somerville, MA: Wisdom Publications, 1997.

Kingsley, Charles. *BrainyQuote.com.* Xplore Inc. 2014. http://www.brainyquote.com/quotes/quotes/c/charleskin393303.html (accessed June 17, 2014).

Weathering Accidental Enlightenment

Kubler-Ross, M.D., Elisabeth. *On Death and Dying.* New York, NY: Scribner, 1969.

Kuhn, Thomas S. *The Structure of Scientific Revolutions.* Second Edition, Enlarged. Chicago: The University of Chicago Press, 1970.

Lama, Dalai. *BrainyQuote.com.* Xplore Inc. 2013. http://www.brainyquote.com/quotes/authors/d/dalai_lama.html (accessed February 25, 2013).

Longfellow, Henry Wadsworth. *The Birds of Killingworth.* Sloan Publishing Company, 1915.

Matisse, Henri. *BrainyQuote.com.* Xplore Inc. 2013. http://www.brainyquote.com/quotes/authors/h/henri_matisse.html (accessed February 25, 2013).

May, Gerald G., M.D. *The Dark Night of the Soul.* Harper One, An Imprint of Harper Collins Publishers, 2004.

VH1 Behind the Music - Meatloaf; Season 1, Episode 16. Produced by VH1 Behind the Music. Performed by Meatloaf. 1998.

Mencius. *The Works of Mencius.* Translated by James Legge. London: Oxford University Press, 1895.

Merriam-Webster. http://merriam-webster.com/dictionary/paradigm (accessed November 16, 2012).

Michelangelo. *BrainyQuote.com.* Xplore Inc. 2013. http://www.brainyquote.com/quotes/quotes/m/michelange108779.html (accessed November 6, 2013).

Miller, Barbara Stoler, trans. *The Bhagavad-Gita.* New York: Bantam Books, 1986.

Monsters, Inc. Produced by Disney Pixar. 2001.

Nordby, Jacob. *The Divine Arsonist.* Boise, ID: Awakened Life Publications, 2012.

O. Carl Simonton, M.D., Stephanie Matthews-Simonton, James L. Creighton. *Getting Well Again.* Bantam edition 1980, Bantam re-issue 1992. New York: Bantam Books, a division of Bantam Doubleday Dell Publishing Group, Inc., 1978.

Paine, Thomas. "Brian Tracy Quote of the Day." *daily e-mail newsletter.* July 16, 2012.
Penney, J. C. "Brian Tracy Quote of the Day." *daily e-mail newsletter.* August 26, 2012.
Pilar Stella, Cynthia Aliza Blake. *BEing the Present: 101 Ways to Inspire Living and Giving.* New York: Morgan James Publishing, 2009.
Plutarch. *BrainyQuote.com.* Xplore Inc. 2014. http://www.brainyquote.com/quotes/quotes/p/plutarch120365.html (accessed February 7, 2014).
Proceedings of the Third Biennial Convention of the Amalgamated Clothing Workers of America. Library of Princeton University, 1919.
Quran.
Rajneesh, Bhagwan Shree. *Wikipedia.* http://en.wikipedia.org/wiki/Bhagwan_Shree_Rajneesh (accessed August 7, 2013).
Robbins, Anthony. Quote of Anthony Robbins used by permission from Robbins Research International, Inc. 2013. http://www.TonyRobbins.com/ (accessed October 30, 2013).
—. *ThinkExist.com.* 2013. http://thinkexist.com/quotation/you-re_in_the_midst_of_a_war-a_battle_between_the/297011.html (accessed March 5, 2013).
Rogers, Fred. *THE WORLD ACCORDING TO MISTER ROGERS: Important Things to Remember.* New York, NY: Hachette Book Group, Inc., 2003.
Rudolph, Wilma. "Bob Proctor's Insight of the Day." *daily e-mail newsletter.* July 5, 2012.
—. "Brian Tracy Quote of the Day." *daily e-mail newsletter.* July 1, 2012.
Rumi. *GoodReads.com.* 2013. http://www.goodreads.com/author/quotes/875661.Rumi (accessed March 5, 2013).

Weathering Accidental Enlightenment

Russell, Bertrand. *SearchQuotes.com*. 2013. http://www.searchquotes.com/quotation/Most_people_would_rather_die_than_think%3B_in_fact,_they_do_so./362242/ (accessed March 5, 2013).

Shakespeare, William. *Hamlet.*

Shaw, George Bernard. *ThinkExist.com*. 2013. http://thinkexist.com/quotation/two_percent_of_the_people_think_three_percent_of/328319.html (accessed March 5, 2013).

Shinn, Florence Scovel. *The Game of Life and How To Play It.* originally published in 1925. New York: Penguin Group, 2009.

Shoaff, John Earl. "How To Become A Millionaire!" *How To Become A Millionaire!* 1962.

Spurgeon, Charles. *GoodReads.com*. 2013. http://www.goodreads.com/quotes/342380-the-man-who-never-reads-will-never-be-read-he (accessed March 3, 2013).

Stephenson, R.W. *Chiropractic Textbook - Volume XIV.* Davenport, IA: The Palmer School of Chiropractic, 1927.

Strang, Virgil V. *Essential Principles Of Chiropractic.* Fifth Printing First Edition 1990. Davenport, IA: Palmer College of Chiropractic, 1984.

—. "Per Dr. Strang's lectures during 9th Trimester Philosophy Class at Palmer College of Chiropractic." Davenport, IA, 1996.

The Princeton Encyclopedia Of Poetry & Poetics. Fourth Edition. New Jersey: Princeton University Press, 2012.

Thoreau, Henry David. *BrainyQuote.com*. Xplore Inc. 2014. http://www.brainyquote.com/quotes/quotes/h/henrydavid120890.html (accessed June 17, 2014).

—. *Walden - Life In The Woods.* 1854.

Tocqueville, Alexis de. *BrainyQuote.com*. Xplore Inc. 2013.

http://www.brainyquote.com/quotes/quotes/a/alexisdeto38 4737.html (accessed November 18, 2013).

Tolle, Eckhart. *Eckhart Tolle Newsletter.* 2011. http://www.eckharttolle.com/newsletter/october-2011 (accessed January 25, 2013).

—. *The Power of Now.* Novato, CA: Publisher's Group West, 1999.

Tree of Life in Bahrain Desert - Faith in Adversity. http://drpaulose.com/spirituality/tree-of-life-in-bahrain-desert-faith-in-adversity (accessed November 26, 2012).

Trine, Ralph Waldo. *In Tune With The Infinite.* Lexington, Kentucky: Seven Treasures Publications, 2009.

Twist, Lynne. *The Soul of Money.* New York: W. W. Norton & Company, 2003.

Tzu, Lao. *Tao Te Ching The Book of the Way.* Translated by Dwight Goddard (1919). Ancient Renewal, 2009.

—. *www.ThinkExist.com.* http://thinkexist.com/quotation/when_i_let_go_of_what_i_am_i_become_what_i_might/340907.html (accessed August 7, 2013).

Tzu, Sun. *The Art of War.* Translated by Griffith, Samuel B. (1963). Oxford: Oxford University Press, 1971.

Valery, Paul. *BrainyQuote.com.* Xplore Inc. 2013. http://www.brainyquote.com/quotes/authors/p/paul_valery.html (accessed October 24, 2013).

Vinci, Leonardo da. "Neale Donald Walsch "I Believe God Wants You To Know"." *daily e-mail newsletter.* November 29, 2011.

Virgil. *SelfGrowth.com.* David Riklan. October 14, 2013. http://www.SelfGrowth.com (accessed October 14, 2013).

Voltaire. *BrainyQuote.com.* Xplore Inc. 2013. http://www.brainyquote.com/quotes/authors/v/voltaire.html (accessed February 25, 2013).

Waitley, Denis. *Denis Waitley International Newsletter.* 2012.

http://go.success.com/deniswaitley/newsletter_archive/2012/8/dw_issue215_web.html (accessed August 21, 2012).

Wall-E. Produced by Disney Pixar. 2008.

Walsch, Neale Donald. "I Believe God Wants You To Know." *daily e-mail newsletter.* April 21, 2011.

—. "I Believe God Wants You To Know." *daily e-mail newsletter.* November 29, 2013.

Wattles, Wallace. *The Science Of Getting Rich.* Tuscon, Arizona: Iceni Books, 2001.

Webster's New Universal Unabridged Dictionary . New York: Random House Value Publishing, Inc., 1996.

West, Morris. *BrainyQuote.com.* Xplore Inc. 2013. http://www.brainyquote.com/quotes/authors/m/morris_west.html (accessed March 3, 2013).

Wikipedia - Dark Night of the Soul. http://en.wikipedia.org/wiki/Dark_Night_of_the_Soul (accessed November 28, 2012).

Wikipedia - Moulting. 2013. http://en.wikipedia.org/wiki/molting (accessed March 4, 2013).

Wikipedia - Wilma Rudolph. http://en.wikipedia.org/wiki/wilma_rudolph (accessed March 4, 2013).

Wikipedia. *Wikipedia.* 2013. http://en.wikipedia.org/wiki/Know_thyself (accessed February 25, 2013).

WikiQuote. http://en.wikiquote.org/wiki/Niels_Bohr (accessed 04 22, 2013).

Oprah's Life Class (with guest Joel Osteen). Produced by OWN Network. Performed by Oprah Winfrey. 2012.

Yosemite's Scenic Wonders Vacation Rentals. http://.scenicwonders.com/california-redwood-trees/ (accessed November 26, 2012).

The Zero's Journey

Weathering Accidental Enlightenment

Notes

Notes

Notes

Weathering Accidental Enlightenment

Notes

The Zero's Journey

Notes

Notes

Notes

Weathering Accidental Enlightenment

Notes

Notes

Weathering Accidental Enlightenment

Notes

Notes